Thomas J.J. Altizer is the author of **The Descent into Hell, The Gospel of Christian Atheism,** and several other books. A leading Christian dialectical theologian, Dr. Altizer is a professor of English and was the first chairman of an interdisciplinary program in religious studies at the State University of New York at Stony Brook. The present volume reflects six years of theological work and may be considered his first major work since **The Descent into Hell.**

D1032244

THE SELF-EMBODIMENT

OF GOD

THE SELF-EMBODIMENT
OF GOD

THOMAS J. J. ALTIZER

Harper & Row, Publishers
New York, Hagerstown,
San Francisco, London

FIRST EDITION

Designed by Janice Stern

Library of Congress Cataloging in Publication Data

Altizer, Thomas J   J
  The self-embodiment of God.
  1. Religion and language. I. Title.
BL65.L2A45   1977   201'.4   76–62952
ISBN 0–06–060160–4

77 78 79 80 81 10 9 8 7 6 5 4 3 2 1

FOR

MOTHER

CONTENTS

THE SELF-EMBODIMENT

OF GOD

INTRODUCTION

Theology today is most fundamentally in quest of a language and mode whereby it can speak. Above all it is in quest of a language whereby it can speak of God. Ever increasingly and decisively this quest is becoming a quest for language itself, and for a new language, a language whereby we can actually and fully speak. Again and again we have discovered that the greatest obstacle to speech about God is now the obstacle of speech itself. If language has become a prison-house in our time, then so likewise has speech. We can speak about God only if we can fully and actually speak, even if such speech should be indirect, paradoxical, or veiled. Yet it is the very possibility of such speech which is most in question for us.

Speech is the most immediate and intimate arena of our life and identity. Whether in interior monologue or in exterior confrontation and response, speech is our primal mode of realizing identity and meaning, and neither meaning nor identity can be actual and real apart from speech. No doubt the uniquely modern obstacles to speech revolve about a breakdown in meaning and identity in the modern world. And this breakdown may be observed not only in society and politics, but also in literature and the arts, as well as in physics and philosophy. Speech has become ever more precarious in all of these realms, and most frequently the actual exercise of speech seems to deepen rather than to resolve this situation.

Yet this situation is analagous to the original situation or situations of biblical faith. Certainly the time of the prophets and the time of the New Testament were times of cultural and historical breakdown, and thus they were times which generated their own deep obstacles to speech. In large measure biblical speech not only arises in but is occasioned by such vacuums. But then so likewise are the great creative breakthroughs of the modern world. Speech arises out of silence and the fullest speech may well arise out of the deepest silence. Certainly genuine speech is inextricably related to silence, which is one reason why genuine speech cannot continue or survive as such in its given or original form and mode. Speech must die to live, and this from moment to moment, and from world to world. But the speech that is born out of death or silence is not simply identical with a previous speech. Inevitably, it is a new speech, and it is new precisely because it is fully speech.

Speech can only be itself by being decisively and actually other than that which it once was or that which it will become. Just as we cannot speak the language of faith by merely repeating the words of faith, then so likewise we cannot actually speak simply by speaking. And that which we actually say will not be that which we said yesterday or a minute ago. So it is that the language of faith can never be the language of yesterday, and above all not when the yesterday of faith is worlds or aeons removed from our world and identity. This is the situation which occasions our crisis of faith, a crisis in which we seem to be incapable of speech.

There is no way out of this crisis until we first acknowledge the crisis itself. And the deeper our sense of crisis the more radical or total will be the turn or movement of speech demanded of us. Our greatest danger is in thinking that faith itself lies outside of our crisis. This is to think that faith lies outside of speech, and therefore outside of all activity and life. Not only does faith then assume a wholly passive identity, but an inhuman and unreal identity as well. Faith then becomes not simple speechlessness but the very absence of all possibility of speech. In short, faith is thereby conceived as either impotence or death.

We will rather think of faith as the fullness of speech. Or as the fullness of that speech which both actualizes and embodies its own ground, its own ultimate or final ground. Then faith will be identified with a speech which is both speech and listening at once. Faith begins as a response to the mystery of speech, or a response to the mystery of the primal ground of speech. But faith is real, or is realized, only insofar as that mystery is spoken, and spoken so as to be heard. And this occurs in hearing a speech which itself impels speech insofar as it is heard. The listening of faith is not a passive listening, it is rather a full and active hearing. That hearing is inseparable from speech, for it says what it hears, and says it so as to make it its own.

This saying is act, an actual act, and an act which actually occurs. The hearing and speaking of faith occur here and now or they do not occur at all. If they occur, they doubtless occur in multiple ways, and in ways continually challenging our understanding. Accordingly, faith may be hidden or disguised, and perhaps most so when it is most fully itself. While our time appears to mark the end of faith, faith may have come to an end in its manifest form only to be reborn in a new form. If this has not yet occurred, it may well be occurring, and occurring wherever speech and hearing are fully actual and real.

In our situation, an act or statement of faith will often not appear to be such at all. So likewise a theological language attempting to understand such an act or statement will seldom present itself in an overtly or manifestly theological language. For little that is overtly theological is actually hearable or speakable today. However, this situation can make possible the realization of a new theological language, a theological language which will speak by way of the voice or the voices of our own time. Voice is not timeless, just as it is not spoken in a void. And in a time when fundamental identities have ever increasingly become unnameable, theological statements can seldom speak in a manifestly theological language. This is not to say that they must necessarily speak in a cryptic language, or even in a language of ciphers. But it is to say that genuine theological statements will surprise both their hearers and their speakers.

That surprise will often occur as a language evolves which conjoins a primal question with a speakable response. Such a response will be spoken in our language, a language which we actually speak, and yet it will truly be a response to a primal and inescapable question. Then that question itself will realize a new form, a form which we can actually hear and speak, and can speak and hear in that language which is actually at hand. Thereby a seemingly unbridgeable chasm between our primal questions and our contemporary speech will be closed, and closed insofar as we can actually hear and speak. Yet if it is so closed, it will be closed in startling ways, for then all distance will have vanished between the language of our primal questions and the language of our actual speech. While such closure may only be momentary, it will be speakable, and hearable as well. Indeed, we will hear that closure insofar as we can speak it, insofar as we can say it ourselves. And when we say it, and as we say it, we will hear a primal question echoing in our own speech.

The great temptation of our time, and temptation to faith itself, is a way of pure and final silence. Silence as silence is prior to speech, and it is not simply the ground out of which speech evolves, it is also that which speech becomes when it ceases to be speech. Silence is both our origin and our end. As our origin, it is the goal of every way which is a way of return. Pure ways of return are ways of eternal return, and ultimately they are ways of pure silence. But silence is also our end, it is the common destiny of us all, and it is our own whether we will it or whether it simply falls upon us. Therefore silence is both the alpha and the omega of speech, it is that ground and end which is the final identity of speech. Silence is that which speech must struggle against to become speech, and yet silence is that which speech inevitably becomes as speech. Speech is speech only because of silence, and yet silence appears to lie wholly beyond all speech.

It is the farness, the beyondness, the pure transcendence of silence which is challenged by the advent of speech. When speech occurs, and as it occurs, the distance of silence becomes near at hand. Then silence is manifest in speech, is speakable in speech, and is so because it is silence itself which passes into speech. Mythically envisioned, the advent of speech is both creation and fall. For speech is simultaneously both the origin of all meaning and identity and a fall from the quiescence and peace of silence. From the perspective of silence, the advent of speech is a rupture, and a primal rupture at that. Indeed, it is the primal rupture, the original source of fall. Hence ways of silence, of pure silence, are intended to annul the advent of speech. Here, voice is silenced, and it is silenced so as to make both possible and necessary the nonbeginning of speech. Such ways are embodied both communally in ritual and interiorly in mysticism, and they most clearly make manifest what we have come to understand in our own time as the primal identity of religion.

Today theology is being challenged as it has never been before by both the power and the seeming inevitability of ways of silence. And this is a challenge to the very foundation of theology, to its very possibility. For theology must simply disappear if silence, or the silence of silence, is the true end of speech. At most it could then be an ancillary discipline, a discipline preparing the way for the end of speech. Such, indeed, it has long since become, at least as it is most commonly practiced today. And not the least reason for this is that the power and the actuality of speech in our time have become so alien to our established theological languages and modes of speech. Yet it is not simply older theologies which are now being challenged and tempted by ways of silence: it is all theology whatsoever. How can theology conjoin speech and hearing if pure silence is the ultimate identity of speech?

This very question allows us to see that theology is a fundamental way by which we can struggle both to maintain and to establish the actuality of speech. As that actuality disappears, so likewise will meaning and identity disappear for us. Then we would truly return to that end which is our beginning, and that return would not be cultic and interior but rather actual and real. Thus theology is one of the great battlegrounds of our time, and it is that ground upon which we must establish the possibility of bringing together or uniting the primal or final identities of both silence and speech. This we cannot do if we refuse or evade the actual speech of our own time and world. Nor can we take up this challenge if we accede to the simple finality of silence. We must rather attempt to establish or understand a dialectic between silence and speech, and a dialectic between the primal identity of silence and the actual and contemporary identity of speech.

This study is a theological reflection upon speech which intends to make manifest the self-actualization of God as the center and ground of our speech and silence. It proceeds by way of a meditative analysis and reenactment of the origin, identity, movement, and actuality of speech. Its intention is to embody the fullness of the biblical movement of faith, and it evolves by way of an evolutionary yet interior movement of the biblical moments and movements of Genesis, Exodus, Judgment, Incarnation, and Apocalypse. The sacred history of the Bible here becomes interiorized and universalized, but interiorized in the moments and movements of our actual consciousness. The fundamental purpose of the book is to open yet another way to a new theological language, a language that will be biblical and contemporary at once and altogether.

Yet the language which is sought here can be real only insofar as it can be actually heard and actually spoken. It can have no meaning or reality apart from the response of the reader, for here the reader is simultaneously listener and speaker, and is fully reader only by being the author or source of what is read. Certainly this book is the product of many speakers and of many listeners as well. Foremost among these were John B. Cobb, Jr. and Ray L. Hart. Invaluable responses were also received from Clayton Carlson, Mircea Eliade, Justus George Lawler, William Mallard, Barbara Sproul, Walter A. Strauss, and Edith Wyschogrod. The book is dedicated to my mother both in gratitude for her presence and in a recognition that insofar as there is a source that source is always in another.

I

GENESIS

What is speech? We ask this question, and ask it again and again, at a time when our speech is seemingly passing into silence, and speech as speech is ever more fully becoming impossible for us. But we have long since learned that questions only truly arise or become overwhelming when they inquire about that which is lost or is disappearing. Inquiry itself, in this perspective, is a response to a newly realized emptiness or void, and when we truly question, we not only evoke but also embody, either an absence or a loss. When we ask about speech we are certainly not engaging in an innocent inquiry, nor can it be a bounded or even a disciplined inquiry. For to ask about speech, and ask fundamentally, is finally to raise every possible question about meaning and identity. Of course, we cannot evoke all such questions in our actual acts or moments of speech. Nevertheless, their absence becomes presence when we inquire about speech, and so much so that our very questioning of speech threatens to pass into silence.

Now silence is not simply and always an absence of speech. Often silence is listening, and therein it is a listening to what is not said, and not said in speech itself. Chatter is simultaneously silence and speech, and its speech is inseparable from its silence, for it is not possible simply to listen to what it says. We enjoy chatter because it is not only speech, it gives us surcease from the presence of speech, and does so by a speech which is both speech and not speech at once. But if chatter speaks only by what it fails to say, it is not silent, and its lack of silence might tell us something about silence itself. Silence can dwell in speech, but its emptiness is negated by the presence of speech. When silence is present in speech it is not a mere emptiness, just as it is not a simple absence, it is far rather a presence, and a presence which is present in the presence of speech. Speech gives this silence its identity, and its meaning as well, for when silence is meaningful it is so only insofar as it is related to speech.

If silence can be present in speech, then so likewise speech is present in silence, and a common dimension of each is made manifest by that which cannot be said. What can we not say? Obviously, we cannot say everything, not even everything which is at hand. A plenum may be evoked by rite or by symbol, but it cannot be spoken, it cannot pass into actual speech. Nor is it accidental that silence is the most cherished language of both mystics and of masters of ritual, for each is in quest of an original ground or source lying on the hither side of speech. It is not possible to speak a plenum, for at most it would be just that, a plenum, and not plenum itself. The very act of speech disjoins the said from the not-said, and hence embodies otherness in its utterance. Speech is the "other" not of silence, but rather of the unsaid, the unnamed, and the unnameable. Plenum or everything is by necessity unsaid and unsayable, for if it were to be spoken, then nothing would be other than speech.

But if everything cannot be spoken, then neither can nothing be said. We must not confuse silence with saying nothing, for silence does not speak, thus it cannot say anything. Nor can speech say nothing, not only in the sense that speech speaks, but also in the sense that it is impossible to say nothing, to speak and say nothing at all.Presence becomes manifest in the very act of speech, and the manifestation of presence makes absence audible. When listening is at hand, as it is in the presence of speech, the inaudible ceases to be silent, or ceases to be a silence which is only silence. While silence alone cannot speak, it ceases to be alone in the presence of speech, and therefore is no longer merely silence. Silence becomes "other" than itself in speech, and thus it ceases to be silence, or ceases to be a silence which is unsaid. Not only is it impossible to speak and say nothing, it is also impossible to speak and hear nothing, for absence as absence comes to an end in the presence of speech.

Now if neither everything nor nothing can be spoken, what does this say about the relation between silence and speech? A total presence, a plenum or totality, becomes disembodied in the embodiment of speech. The act of speech is just that, an act or utterance, and as act it is actual, it is present, and present alone, in its own embodiment. But it can be so present, so actually present, only through the absence of a total presence or totality. Hence speech as speech can be present only through the presence of silence. The infinite must be silent before speech can be at hand, for in the presence of the infinite, speech cannot speak. Therefore silence is necessary to speech, for apart from silence there could be no speech, no actual speech, no speech which speaks. Yet speech is also necessary to silence, for apart from speech silence would be absent, as silence is only present in the presence of speech. Accordingly, silence and speech are necessary to each other, and each apart from the other cannot be itself.

Silence is not the unsaid, or not the unsaid in speech, in that speech which actually speaks. The unsaid and the unsayable are truly the "other" of speech, they are that which speech ceases to be when it is spoken. Once speech speaks, it not only ceases to be unsaid, it becomes itself its own negation of the unsaid. The voice of speech is not the voice of silence, it is the voice of its own self-negation, of its negation of itself as unspoken. This is the source of the immediacy of speech, of its presence or actuality. True, speech is not always immediate, it may be, and commonly is, only partially and indirectly present. Nevertheless, whatever is present in speech derives only from itself, from its own act or embodiment. And that act, precisely because it is only its own, is an act of self-negation. The unsaid is not simply inactive or nonactual speech, it is speech which is "other" than itself, speech, which in not having been spoken, is actually the other of speech. Therefore the unsaid becomes "other" than itself in being spoken. And thereby it truly becomes its own "other," it negates itself in speech, and only by negating itself does it become embodied or present.

Speech, in this perspective, is self-division. It becomes divided from itself in being spoken, and divided from itself as unspoken. The real unsaid is not simply the unspoken, it is rather that which is left behind as the "other" of speech. The act of speech is self-embodiment, and it embodies itself by negating itself, by dividing itself from itself. So it is that the presence of voice is always an absence, an absence of itself as the unsaid, and a loss of itself as the unsayable. Once voice is present or embodied, that loss is irrevocable, it can never be annulled by a turn of speech, or even by a movement into silence. For once speech is spoken, or is self-embodied, its own unsaid becomes truly "other," and truly other than itself. The act of speech seals, and definitively seals, the division of speech from itself as the unsaid, and the estrangement of speech from itself as the unsayable. Accordingly, the self-embodiment of speech is a self-doubling, a doubling wherein the sayable and the unsayable become the intrinsic others of each other. Apart from the intrinsic otherness of the said and the unsaid, speech would have no ground upon which to stand, no ground whereby it could be present and manifest as speech.

Innocence is lost with the advent of speech, and eternally lost, unless speech can return to its origin in the unsaid.

There can be no innocent speech, this is an illusion sustained by those who are closed to the power of speech, or who refuse to attend to the presence of speech. The very presence of speech establishes distance as well as intimacy, a distance deriving from the act of speech, an act wherein speech stands out from itself, and in standing out from itself it embodies its distance from itself in its own voice. Voice speaks, and in speaking it startles, it calls attention to itself, and its calling can only be heard over distance. This distance arises from the chasm now established between the said and the unsaid, but so likewise does it arise from the direction of speech itself. That direction initially lies outside the speaker, and this is an outside arising from the doubling of speech, a doubling establishing not only the actuality of speech, but also a separation between speaker and listener. This separation is not simply a distinction, it is rather a division, a division between the act of speech and the silence of listening, between the nearness of voice and the farness of listening.

Distance and intimacy are mutually established by speech, but they are established not as distinct and isolated fields, but rather as mutual and ever-present poles of one continuum. While neither can be fully or wholly distinguished from the other in the presence of speech, it is also true that each remains itself in the act or embodiment of speech, for so long as speech speaks both distance and intimacy are maintained by the presence and actuality of voice. Communion or coinherence may be realized by the act of speech, but never union or identity. Union and identity are realized only by silence, never by speech, and speech can only prepare the way for union by ever more fully ceasing to speak. So long as speech speaks distance is at hand, and at hand not simply in its distinction from silence, but also in the very intimacy which its voice establishes. To listen to speech, as opposed to listening to silence, is to be open to otherness, an otherness impossible apart from distance, and an otherness which is real only in the context of distance. Yet the otherness established by speech is not an empty or vacuous otherness. It is far rather a present and actual otherness, even an intimate otherness, an otherness which is not only distant and apart but which is likewise and simultaneously near at hand.

Speech may be hollow, but it is never formless or boundless or without a center which is somewhere. That somewhere may be nowhere to the listener, but it is never everywhere, for speech is not only act but also embodiment. When speech speaks, distance is not only established, but it is established as intimate presence, a presence wherein the otherness of distance becomes audible and manifest. Such otherness is audible not simply in its presence, for silence is present, but also in its immediacy, in the force and even violence of its presence. For speech not only startles, it also assaults, it assaults that presence which its own voice establishes, and so much so that the presence of voice is inseparable from violence. We are not commonly aware of the violence of speech, but we have only to compare the tones of silence and speech to recognize that violence; for silence is not without its own tone, a tone that is indispensable to the tonalities of voice. The violence of speech is inseparable from the immediacy of speech, voice calls, and its call is immediate, its calling assaulting its hearer so as to transform the distance of listening into nearness. Apart from violence speech might be unheard, its immediacy might be present only to itself, and its voice might be a soliloquy.

But soliloquis are always silent, they can never be spoken or pronounced; for once they are spoken they cease to be silent and alone, and invoke instead a presence which is never solitary. When voice speaks, response is not only near at hand, it is immediate; for voice cannot speak without inevitably and immediately evoking a response. Response may be silent, of course, but it is nevertheless a response, a reaction to speech. Yet response cannot be innocent, or only so in its manner, never in its tone. Not only can response not evade the violence of speech, it must also embody it, for the force of speech is not consumed in speaking, it rather confronts and assaults its listener. So it is that a response to voice can never be merely quiescent or passive, just as it cannot be solitary and alone; for voice banishes privacy and solitude, and does so by the violence of its assault. Not only is solitude negated by speech, but so likewise is stillness and calm and tranquility. Who can be innocent in the presence of speech?

When we respond to speech, we are aware, even if only implicitly, of being drawn not to the speaker, but rather to the speaker's voice. That voice rivets our attention, indeed, it creates it, and creates it in such a manner as to direct it only to itself. True, we may evade the call of voice, but never can we do so spontaneously, and never with even the semblance of grace. If voice is not always grave, it always embodies gravity, and that gravity is its own; it resides in the actuality of voice. Once hearing voice, we are startled away from weightlessness; or away from a sensibility knowing neither weight nor weightlessness. The air becomes heavy in the presence of voice, or it ceases to be weightless, ceases to be light, and innocent, and free. For the very advent of voice transforms sameness into difference and identity into otherness. Once voice has spoken, a center sounds or is manifest, and it appears or names itself as center and source, and that naming, that sounding, can only name or sound by distancing itself from its hearer. While voice's distance may be present in nearness, and indeed is, it nevertheless is truly distant, and is distant precisely in its nearness. The presence of such a distant, a forceful and violent presence, disrupts the presence in its midst, transforming that presence into absence. Not into an empty or vacuous absence to be sure, but into an absence nonetheless, an absence from that silence which is closed to speech. In the presence of speech, silence can be present only to the extent that it is no longer simply itself.

While silence may maintain itself in the presence of speech, it can no longer sustain itself only as silence, just as it can no longer be calm or still. Silence becomes other than itself in the presence of speech, it becomes different from itself, but it nevertheless remains itself in that difference, if only because it doesn't speak. Now silence is identical with itself only in its difference, in its difference from itself as a silence which is simply silence. By this difference from itself silence becomes actually and immediately present, thereby echoing that voice to which it is called. If speech is embodied, a silence which is other than itself is embodied, too, and embodied by virtue of its very difference from itself as a quiescent silence. Now silence listens, but it doesn't simply listen, it listens to voice. And it can listen to voice only because it is now other than itself, it is no longer quiescent and alone. Perhaps attention is present in an original silence, but it is not an attending to, for it is without direction or intention. Now silence has both an intention and a direction, even if it intends to evade the call of voice. Therein silence acts, and it actually acts, it embodies itself in a presence which is not its own.

Speech, too, becomes other than itself when it is spoken, or actually different from itself as a mere possibility of speech. When voice sounds, it is thrown into a new presence, and a presence which is truly different from the presence of unspoken speech. Voice jars, it bursts forth, and it bursts forth in an immediate presence which is overwhelming, so overwhelming that it cannot, in its immediate presence, be annulled. In that immediacy, voice cannot be annulled by either speaker or listener, nor can its presence as voice be either forgotten or erased. Once voice has spoken, its speech can never be re-called, and perhaps it is just because it cannot be re-called that the presence of speech is so compelling. Therein speech is once again decisively different from the unsaid, and even from itself as unsaid, so different, indeed, that the voice of speech is wholly other than the silence of the unsaid.

This is so because the unspoken is without actuality, iso-

15

lated from all response, it is a mere passivity. Like the plenum which can reside only in an original silence, it is actually different from nothing whatsoever, and is identical only with itself. But when speech speaks, or voice bursts forth, actuality is established. Moreover, it is established with such finality that an identity which is only itself is wholly left behind. For the presence of speech is not identical with itself, or its identity derives from its difference from itself, a difference wherein its presence is not simply its own. Here, presence calls, and it calls to itself, but the voice which calls is not only itself, it calls wherever it is embodied. Voice is omnipresent in its domain, hence it is not only itself, it acts and is actual wherever it is heard. This is not to say that voice is without a center or a source, but it is to say that voice is voice in its speech, and here it is embodied with such finality that it is present nowhere else. When speech speaks, the unsaid is unheard and unrecognizable, and is so even in the silence which it evokes. Not only is it unheard, but it is also unmanifest, and totally unmanifest, so much so that voice as voice is inherently "other" than the unsaid and the unnameable.

The actuality of speech is inescapable, for it is present wherever it is heard, and it is heard wherever its voice is present. Once speech has spoken, its voice establishes a world or a field, and that field is indissoluble, it cannot simply disappear or pass away. True, it may no longer be heard, or no longer heard in its original domain, but its effect can never be erased, its act never undone. There is a finality in speech which is inseparable from its act, a finality making manifest the ultimacy of act itself, for once act has been embodied or enacted it can never thereafter simply pass away or come to an end. While speech can be remembered it can never be re-called, it can never cease to be speech, never cease to be itself. Thus the unsaid becomes other than itself in speech, and wholly other, for speech brings a definitive and final end to the pure silence and passivity of the unnamed and the unsaid. And this it does in its very actuality, in its actually having been spoken, in its having been said.

Not only is speech the absence of the unsaid, but it enacts a total negation of the unsaid, it embodies the pure otherness of the unsaid. In that otherness we can detect a significant meaning of actuality, for actuality is the pure otherness of the inactive and unrealized. Actuality does not simply express or realize the nonactual, it rather negates it, and it negates it so as to realize the nonactual as the intrinsic otherness of itself. This is why the presence of speech is not simply different from a disembodied silence, it is its integral and intrinsic negation, a negation wherein an undifferentiated silence becomes the opposite of itself. Now presence is neither everywhere nor nowhere, it is concretely and actually present, it is present here and now.

Consequently, the presence established by speech is wholly other than what we might imagine as the omnipresence of an eternal now. In this perspective we can see that not only could an eternal now not actually exist, but that whatever "isness" it might embody is the opposite of actuality, the opposite of the actual presence of embodiment. When speech speaks it acts, and it acts in its actuality, in its actual presence. There is a fullness in speech which is the opposite of the silence of the unsaid, and its actual opposite, its real negation. Speech is not simply the absence of the unsaid, it is its actual negation, its real opposite. A real opposite, that is an actual and concrete opposite, must not be confused with a polar opposite or contrary. A contrary, or polar opposite, is an opposite in character or in nature, or in position or direction, which is integral to or inherent in its own opposite, and is so continually, and in a never-changing manner and mode. But a real and actual opposite is so only as a consequence of an act of negation. Such an act is not and cannot be a continual and eternal act or action. It is far rather the opposite of an eternal act, and the real opposite, for the act of negation is an actual act, and it is actual because it actually negates.

The omnipresent silence of the unsaid is actually negated by speech, and this is a real negation, for once it has occurred an original quiescence or silence is no more, or is no more within the horizon or the echo of the embodiment of voice. The presence of voice embodies the final loss of an original silence, once voice speaks quiescence can never return, for the presence of voice is possible only by way of an actual negation of the unsaid. Voice can be heard only with and through the dissolution of quiescence, and that dissolution is not an eternal process, it is an actual dissolving, an actual end of an original or eternal silence. But if speech ends an original silence, and actually ends it, then the advent of speech is a beginning. Moreover, it is an actual beginning, a real beginning, a beginning which is the real opposite of a continual and eternal quiescence. When speech speaks, sound sounds, voice is embodied, and actuality is present, and it is present here and now. Yet voice is the embodiment of a negation of a quiescent silence, and the hither side of that negation is a beginning, a beginning which is the end of innocence, the end of the omnipresence of a plenum or an eternal now.

A beginning? Yes, a beginning because it is an ending, an actual ending of its real opposite, and thus an actual beginning. Actuality itself is unreal apart from a real beginning, for apart from a beginning the actual would be nonactual, or it would be an actual which is simply identical with its nonactual pole or contrary. Such an actual could not act, or it could not act concretely, nor could it be actually present, for then its presence would be identical with its absence. A real beginning is not an eternal beginning, just as a real ending is not an eternal return. Beginning begins, and when it actually begins it embodies the opposite of that which it ends. Hence an actual beginning explodes, and explodes in violence, for it is the opposite of an original stillness.

Once beginning has actually begun a silent and unmoving eternity or plenitude is no more, and is no more by virtue of the advent of beginning. In this sense beginning begins once, and begins only once, for an original stillness or silence can end only once and no more. Once voice has spoken, and has been heard, its hearer cannot return to a quiescent moment prior to the advent of voice, for voice brings all quiescence to an end. Voice violently hurls us away from the plentitude of the unsaid, and does so whether we hear or speak it. In hearing voice we therein cease to hear stillness, cease to be present to stillness, for then the only silence which is present is a silence which is integrally and actually related to speech. Voice embodies a fall from stillness, and a catastrophic fall, a once and for all fall, a fall that can never disappear or be annulled. We may be silent in the presence of voice, but we cannot be still, and having heard voice we can never return to stillness, can never return to a state wherein there is no distinction between the presence and the absence of speech.

Difference becomes actual with the advent of speech, even as identity ceases to be all comprehending, and the presence of an actual difference inaugurates the presence of embodiment. Embodiment is presence, but it is a presence which is an actual absence, the real absence of a simple or total identity. Only the negation of such a total identity or plenitude can establish the possibility of a real and actual act, but such a negation does not simply establish the possibility of act, it rather embodies it, and embodies it as act itself. For embodiment is itself the negation of plenitude, just as it is the negation of stillness and calm, for embodiment is either actually present and real or actually absent and unreal. There can be no simple possibility of embodiment, no embodiment which simultaneously can be present and absent or real and unreal at once. And this is so quite simply because embodiment is either actual or it is nothing at all.

Speech is embodiment, and it is embodied in its act, an act which having been enacted can never be undone. The actuality of speech resides in its finality, for in having been said it has finally been said and nothing can bring its advent to an end. Speech begins, and in having begun it is different from the unsaid, and different just because it begins. For the unsaid cannot begin, even if it comes to an end in speech, and this difference between the impossibility of a beginning of the unsaid and its actual ending in speech makes manifest a decisive meaning of the beginning of speech. The beginning of speech is total, if it is present it is present altogether, and therein it is altogether different from the nonbeginning of the unsaid. The totality of the beginning of speech is the totality of actuality, a totality that must begin and whose beginning releases its actuality. Beginning is actual, it actually begins, and in actually beginning it negates its ground in the nonbeginning of a quiescence which is eternally the same.

Therefore speech is the "other" of an identity which is only itself. That is to say it is the "other" of simple identity, the "other" of an identity which is eternally the same. Speech is difference, it is actually different, and it is actually different from the same. When speech speaks, difference is embodied, and it is actually embodied in the presence of voice. Apart from the distance established by voice, speech could not speak; but this distance is a difference, a difference from an eternal and unmoving identity which is only and totally itself. That identity is not only negated by the advent of speech, it is finally and irrevocably dissolved, and so much so that once speech has spoken a total identity can neither be remembered nor recalled. Speech can speak only by "forgetting," only by forgetting the identity of the same, for apart from the establishment of an actual difference there could be no embodiment of voice.

But speech is not only different from the unsaid, it is totally different, and therein it is even different from itself. The unsaid is simply identical with itself, is eternally the same as itself; but speech can have nothing of this identity, and cannot if only because it actually speaks. The advent of speech shatters, it shatters the stillness of the unsaid, and it shatters because it is different, and its difference lies immediately in itself. Not only is the violence of speech "other" than the stillness of the unsaid, it is also other than itself, for only an integral otherness can shatter and disperse the original quiescence of calm. This is so because an otherness which is not a whole and total otherness could not totally negate the same, could not bring the identity of the same to a decisive and definitive end. A total otherness must be other than itself, it can have nothing within it which is the same as itself, otherwise it would not be total. So it is that the voice of speech is other than speech itself, is other than its own voice, and it is just this otherness which is embodied in the act of speech.

Speech cannot assault stillness, for stillness ends in the presence of speech, it is only that silence which is inseparable from itself which the act of speech can assault. Speech cannot ravage another which is only another, for the immediacy of its act cannot be isolated from itself, cannot be other than itself. Speech wounds, yes, but it also wounds itself, indeed, it inevitably wounds itself, and wounds itself by speaking itself. If the act of speech is a violent act, and act itself is violent in its actuality, then the speech of speech must violate itself, and violate itself in its own embodiment. Hence speech which is speech can never be calm, can never be unmoving or itself unmoved. Its very identity as speech embodies it as the "other" of itself, and the act of that "other" must simultaneously be both for and against itself. Only by being against itself can speech be for itself, and only by negating itself can speech continue to speak.

Accordingly, the continuity of speech is an illusion, or it is an illusion if it is understood or apprehended as an undifferentiated continuum, a continuum which does not embody a difference from itself. The field of speech is a discrete and therefore noncontinuous continuum, a continuum which is other than itself, and other than itself precisely because it is itself. All speech is definite and individual, and thus it is not the same as all other speech, for it is only itself. Speech is itself only by being other than itself, and only by embodying its difference from itself does speech maintain its difference from everything else. That difference is only deepened by the continuity of speech, thus the continuity of speech is the opposite of an undifferentiated or continual continuum, for its continuity not only expresses but embodies difference, and that difference is a real and actual difference, a difference so actual that here continuity can be continuous only when it is discontinuous with itself. That discontinuity is the source of the unique individuality of speech, an individuality deriving from the difference of speech from itself.

Difference is actual, and the difference in speech is embodied in the actuality of speech, an immediate actuality wherein speech is ever and continually different from itself. That difference can also be identified as uniqueness, for uniqueness is only itself, and it itself only by being other than itself. For in being different from everything else, uniqueness is wholly other than the same, but it can only be wholly other than the same by being "other" than itself as the same. A unique presence is the presence of the "other," an other that is itself only by being other, for its otherness is simply and immediately itself. The presence of the "other" embodies difference, and embodies difference in its very presence, a presence wherein otherness is actual and immediate. Not only is such presence overwhelming, it is also unique, and unique in its actual and immediate identity, an identity which can be nothing else. Nothing else that is but itself, and it is precisely by being nothing else that it is itself, for here being nothing else is the actuality of presence itself.

Speech is itself only in its otherness, and not only in its otherness from the other, but also in its otherness from itself. Thus speech not only negates the unsaid, it also negates itself, and negates itself as the other of the unsaid, for only thereby can it continue to speak. Not only is the presence of voice unique, it is unique from moment to moment; thus its presence is not only different, it is continually different, and continually different from itself. If every voice is unique, then so likewise is every moment of voice unique, and is so because voice continually becomes other than itself in every act or moment of speech. Furthermore, the uniqueness of voice derives only from itself, it comes from no other, or rather it comes only from the otherness of itself. That otherness is in itself, and not only is it in itself, it is itself, and is itself as the otherness of itself. In speech difference is embodied in itself, and embodied in itself as itself, for speech is the actual immediacy of a difference which is ever other than itself.

Difference speaks in speech, and it speaks itself, it embodies itself in an actual and immediate presence which is only its own. That presence is a demanding presence, and demanding not simply because it is call, but because it is a call embodying the otherness of itself. One cannot passively attend to speech, or be innocently attentive in the presence of speech, for speech startles, and in startling it disrupts, disrupting not only the stillness of the silence which is its echo, but also the very presence which is established by its voice. That presence can never be calm or still, nor can it simply be itself, for the presence evoked by voice is bound to voice itself. The call of voice commands, and commands by its very presence; but its command cannot be dissociated from its presence, for it is embodied in the immediate actuality of voice. Voice is another, but it is another which is itself. For voice is the presence of that other which is itself only in being other, and only by being other than itself.

We cannot even imagine a voice which has no beginning, nor can we name or envision speech itself as an eternal or unchanging act. On the contrary, simply to name speech is to think of beginning, and to think of beginning as a primal and inescapable identity of speech. In the presence of speech, presence itself is inseparable from beginning, for the presence embodied by speech inescapably and irrevocably begins. And it actually begins, it is manifest in and by way of its beginning, for apart from its beginning it would be neither an actual nor an embodied presence. An embodied presence does not simply signal the advent of beginning, it embodies it, and embodies it in the immediate presence of actuality. Thus the advent of speech is not simply the beginning of speech, it is the actualization of beginning, the embodiment of beginning itself. Once speech has spoken, beginning itself begins, and begins as a total and irrevocable act.

Indeed, the advent of speech is the naming of beginning, and the naming of beginning sets beginning apart from itself. The naming of beginning makes beginning manifest, and makes it manifest as beginning, as ground. Now beginning is manifest as origin, and not as origin which is only itself, but rather as origin which cannot rest in itself, whose end lies in moving beyond itself. Thus the end of speech does not lie in its beginning. That is precisely what we cannot say of speech. And we cannot say it because we cannot speak of an origin which is only a beginning, cannot name an origin whose end lies solely and only in itself. In speech beginning perishes as an eternal beginning, it comes to an end as a beginning which is only a beginning, and becomes actual as an origin which is becoming other than itself.

An origin whose end lies beyond itself is directed against itself, for in being impelled beyond itself it can only be against itself, thus it can be for itself only by being against itself. When origin becomes manifest, it becomes manifest as being beyond itself, as being other than itself. Then beginning speaks, and it actually speaks, it questions. Speech questions when it makes its beginning manifest, then it speaks beyond itself, speaks against itself. Questioning is speech which embodies the origin of speech, which makes manifest the beginning of speech, and does so by a speech which stands forth only by not standing at all. When the beginning of speech is manifest, otherness is at hand, and at hand in the voice of speech itself. Then speech becomes precarious, it makes manifest its own ground, a ground lying beyond the sayable, beyond the possibility of speech itself. But it is not wholly beyond it. For speech speaks, and it speaks in questioning, it speaks even when it embodies its own otherness, and does so by speaking the unsayable. The unsayable becomes spoken when the ground of speech becomes manifest, for even if that ground is beyond speech, it is nevertheless present and actual in speech, and that presence becomes manifest when the otherness of the origin of speech is spoken.

That otherness speaks when beginning speaks, and it speaks in the voice of speech itself, in the actuality of the presence of speech. The presence of actuality, or its actual and immediate presence, impels a recognition of that otherness, for the actual is actual only in its otherness, only in its otherness from that identity which is simply and only itself. If the actual was simply and only itself then it could not be actual, for then it could stand out from nothing whatsoever, and hence it could not stand, it could not become manifest. But the actual as actual is the manifest, it does stand out, it exists, and it exists in its pure immediacy. Nevertheless, that immediacy is not a simple immediacy, not an immediacy that simply exists, it rather ex-ists, it stands out from itself in its presence. Hence an actual immediacy embodies an actual otherness, an otherness which is embodied in voice, and embodied in the actual and immediate otherness of voice.

The actuality of speech embodies a presence which is other than itself, and in being other than itself it cannot rest in itself, it cannot simply be itself, and thereby it embodies itself in a questioning of itself. Questioning is possible only in the presence of rupture, but in the presence of rupture questioning is not simply possible, it is actual, and it is actual because rupture cannot rest. The absence of questioning witnesses to the presence of calm, but calm ends with the advent of speech, and finally ends, and with that ending questioning is embodied, and therein is irrevocably real. Speech questions, its very presence brings an end to an identity which is only itself, but that ending is the beginning of questioning, and so much so that now questioning is simply identical with identity itself. The question that we must ask in the presence of speech is why do we ask at all? Can we not remain silent in the presence of speech? Of course, we cannot, and we cannot because speech is speech, because the presence of speech brings an end to silence, brings an end to that silence which is only itself.

If speech is the actual and immediate presence of a self-embodied otherness, then why is there any speech at all, why not far rather simply silence? Now this is a question which cannot be asked in the presence of speech, for speech brings an end to the very possibility of an original and total silence, thus in the presence of speech that silence cannot even be evoked, much less inveighed as an actual possibility. The silence of silence comes to an end in the presence of speech, as the actuality of speech shatters silence, embodying in its pure otherness a silence which is the other of itself. Silence cannot simply be silent in the presence of speech, for silence speaks in the voice of speech, and speaks in that self-negating otherness which embodies itself in its own otherness. Silence as silence is absent in speech, but silence is present as the "other" of speech, and in that presence it embodies a new identity of itself. Accordingly, in the presence of speech we can only ask about a silence which is other than itself, and other than itself precisely in its presence in speech. Consequently, we can respond to silence in the presence of speech by saying, and only by saying: In the beginning God.

II

EXODUS

God? How can we pronounce the name of God in speaking of silence? But a better question would be can we actually speak any other name in speaking of the origin of the real and actual opposite of speech? An opposite in this sense is not to be confused with that which is simply other. Thus the silence which is present in the presence of speech is not to be identified with the unsaid, the unnamed, or the unnameable, and cannot be so identified if only because silence is present in the voice of speech. Then it is actually present, and actually present in its difference from itself as the unsaid, as its actuality negates the presence of an original and total silence. That silence disappears in the presence of speech, it is inaudible, and is inaudible because it simply is not there. Now this is something which can be said about an original and total silence, it is really absent from speech. Not only is it really absent, it is actually absent, and the actuality of its absence is embodied in the voice of speech.

We hear that absence in the voice of speech, for in the presence of speech it is not possible to listen to nothing at all. Our silence ends with the advent of speech, and truly ends, for once we have heard the voice of speech we can never thereafter be open or awake to a silence which is only silence.

That silence ends in the voice of speech, and with it ends all possibility of listening to nothing, and so likewise ends all possibility of not listening at all. The presence of speech embodies an exile from silence, an exile from that silence which is simply and only itself. That exile is real, actually and audibly real, and we realize it whenever we either listen or speak. But to realize that exile is to name it, even if only implicitly or indirectly, for the exile which is present in the presence of speech is spoken in the voice of speech itself. And not only in the voice of speech, but also in the silence of speech, inasmuch as that silence embodies the end of silence itself.

Silence speaks in the voice of speech, but in that voice it enters into exile from itself, thereby becoming exiled from the silence of itself. Consequently, an exiled silence is not and cannot be a silent or unnameable silence. Silence names itself in its exile from itself, and names itself in realizing or releasing itself in speech. Once speech has spoken, silence is named, and named in its very nakedness, a nakedness in which silence is no longer alone, in which it is no longer only itself. Just as nakedness appears, so does a new silence speak, and it speaks in its emptiness, a new emptiness in which total silence disappears. That is the disappearance which is realized in speech, and it is also realized in that silence which is present in the presence of speech, a silence embodying the disappearance of a silence which is simply and only itself. Silence names itself by ending as silence, and it names itself by embodying the end of silence. Yet how can we speak of the end of silence without thereby speaking of God?

To speak of silence naming itself by ending as silence is to speak of the voice of silence, a voice which silence acquires with the advent of speech, for if silence remains omnipresent its center is no longer everywhere, it is rather embedded in the voice of speech itself. Now silence acquires a center, and with that acquisition silence becomes world, the world established by speech. Without that world silence is solitary and alone, and unspoken and unheard. But with that world silence not only gains a new identity, it becomes other than itself, it realizes itself by becoming exiled from itself. We realize that exile whenever we speak or listen, therein exile becomes embodied in our listening and speech, and this embodiment is not fortuitous, it is an inescapable destiny, a destiny that is present in the actuality of presence itself. Actuality banishes an original silence, and once it is at hand it is ineradicable, as its occurrence is a final and once and for all event. Simply having said this, however, we have named God, for we have spoken of an absolute beginning which can never be annulled. God is the name of absolute beginning, or the name of the source and ground of that beginning, a name which we must name in speaking of the advent of speech. But if God is the name of the source and ground of an absolute or final beginning, this is a name which can only be pronounced on the hither side of that beginning, and only in that exile which this beginning releases and enacts.

If we pronounce the name of God in speaking of beginning, an absolute or final beginning, then the name which we pronounce bears the imprint of that beginning, and thereby it is a name of that which is in exile from itself. Of course, every name which we pronounce bears that imprint, but God is the name of names, the name of the source of names, the name of the source and the ground of absolute beginning. Thus God is the name of exile, the name of the ground of exile, the name of the source of that exile which realizes itself by becoming exiled from itself. Simply by naming God we make that exile manifest, but so likewise is exile manifest in speech, and manifest in that silence which is inseparable from speech. Yet the name of God makes exile manifest in its source, and thereby in its finality, a once and for all finality eradicating every possibility of the nonbeginning of actuality. And to speak the name of God is not simply to speak the name of the ground of actuality, it is to sanction actuality, it is to speak that name whose utterance seals the finality of the actual. Once the name of God has been pronounced, and actually pronounced, then the finality of beginning is not only evoked, it is embodied, and embodied in the presence and the actuality of speech.

Or, rather, the utterance of the name of God makes manifest the ground of actuality, its final ground, its finality. It makes visible, or audible, the final exile of actuality from eternal presence, from a presence whose center is everywhere, and whose source is nowhere. God is the name of the end of eternal presence, and of the beginning of a final exile from that presence, an exile which itself is present only in the utter disappearance of eternal presence. Now eternal presence is not only silent, it is unnameable, and unnameable in the actuality of speech. But in becoming unnameable, and actually unnameable, the end of silence is the beginning of speech, and the final beginning, the beginning of a speech which cannot be unsaid. That beginning is exile, and final exile, an exile wherein identity becomes other than itself, and other than itself in the actuality of speech. By speaking the name of God we make manifest the final exile of speech, thereby we evoke the finality of its ground, and embody in that utterance a naming of the finality of actuality itself.

Once the ground of actuality has been so named, it has been revealed in its finality, and revealed in a finality wherein it can never cease to be itself. But actuality can only be itself by being other than itself, by being other than an identity which is simply itself, and simply itself whenever and wherever it is present. Simple identity is omnipresence, a presence which is everywhere, and which is everywhere itself. Actual presence, to the contrary, is not everywhere, and it is not everywhere precisely because of its actuality, because it is actually present. Only by not being everywhere can actuality be present, be actual, and only be being exiled from itself as an omnipresence can actuality dawn or begin. God is the name of that beginning, or of its ground, and the finality of that name unveils the finality of the actual, a finality apart from which actuality could not begin or be at hand. Yet actuality is at hand, and at hand in speech, and by actually being there it embodies its otherness in itself. To say that otherness is there, finally and ineradicably there, is to speak of God, the God who is the source and the ground of the beginning or dawning of otherness.

We cannot speak of otherness, or of its ground, its final ground, without speaking of God. By speaking of God we speak of the finality of otherness, of an otherness that will ever be other than itself. Actuality is that otherness, but only by speaking of God can we make manifest the finality of that otherness, a finality that is sealed, is sanctioned, when the name of God is spoken. All speech embodies otherness, makes otherness actually present; but only speech about God makes otherness manifest as world, and as the world of actuality. Once the name of God is spoken, that world is manifest as one world, and as the one world in which all worlds are present. To speak of God is to sanction that world, and finally to sanction it, to name it as a finality that can never return to its source. God is the name of the finality of the world of actuality, and when we pronounce that name we speak that finality, we bless it, and we bless it by saying God.

We can say God only by embodying exile in our voice, only by making openly manifest our exile from eternal silence and eternal presence, an original presence which is everywhere, and which is everywhere the same. We acknowledge the disappearance of that presence when we say God, and by saying God we sanction that disappearance, and thereby embody in our own voice our estrangement from an omnipresent and eternal now. God is the name of the source or the origin of our estrangment from the silence of eternal presence. By speaking that name, we negate such silence, or embody in our voice an original negation of that silence, a negation bringing an end to the silence of silence. Therewith likewise ends a presence which is only presence, a presence which is not the otherness of itself, but which is simply and only itself. Now presence is another, it is otherness itself, and presence can be present only by being different from itself.

Speech speaks in the presence of that otherness, an otherness which it embodies in itself, and this is no less true when the name of God is spoken. Accordingly, the God who is spoken or who is named is an embodiment of otherness. And insofar as God is named as God, the source of otherness is named. Thereby is likewise named the ground of all that identity which can never be simply and only itself. So it is that when God is named as God, God is named as the God who is in exile, the God who is in exile from himself. The God who is named, the God who is spoken, is, and immediately is, only insofar as He is other than Himself. Apart from the manifestation of that otherness, God could not be manifest; for only otherness can be manifest, just as only difference can be named. But God is manifest, and manifest when His name is spoken, when speech makes manifest its final ground, and its final ground in otherness. Then silence is impossible, or impossible as a silence which is only itself. God is the name of the end of silence, its final end, and once the name of God has been spoken silence can never again be simply silence. To pronounce the name of God is to embody otherness, to embody the final otherness of both silence and speech, and once that name has been uttered or said the unsaid not only disappears but comes to an end. And it comes to an end in the beginning of speech, its actual beginning, a beginning embodying otherness as identity itself.

In the horizon of speech, and in the horizon of the world embodied in speech, otherness is world, the world of actuality. Thus to speak of God is not only to speak of otherness, it is to embody it, and to embody it in the identity of the God whose name is spoken and pronounced. Within this horizon, the horizon of actual speech, it is not possible simply to speak of the divine, or of a nameless holiness or divinity. And this is true because speech is speech, it is actual speech, it is spoken. To speak of a nameless divinity would be to speak of nothing at all, or of nothing actual, and this is just what actual speech cannot do. Visionaries may dream of a divinity whose circumference is everywhere and whose center is nowhere, but they cannot speak it, and this because speech is actual, it brings an end to an identity which is eternally the same. To speak of God is to speak of otherness, of a final otherness, an otherness which is the same only insofar as it is other. Only in being other is a final otherness itself. Here otherness is the same only in its otherness from itself. That otherness can be spoken, it is spoken in actual speech, and so much so that all actual speech about divinity openly and manifestly embodies otherness.

If actual speech about divinity openly embodies otherness, then the divinity of which it speaks is not nameless, and not nameless because it is manifest in speech as an actual otherness. Silence may evoke a nameless divinity, but it cannot do so within the presence or the horizon of speech, and this because the advent of speech brings the unsaid and the nameless to an end. Once voice has spoken, the silence of the unnamed is no more, and truly is no more, as that silence is finally ended. Now silence speaks, and it speaks in the world of speech, a world in which silence gains a new identity, a world wherein silence cannot simply and only be itself. Such silence also speaks whenever the name of God is spoken, and that silence embodies otherness, an otherness making manifest the identity of the God whose name is pronounced. The only God who can be named is the God who is finally other, for God is other in being named, and God is finally other in being named as God.

To speak of God is to speak of the God who is finally other, finally and wholly other, and finally other than Himself. Only by being other than Himself can God be finally other, for only by being other than Himself can God lose, and finally lose, an identity which is eternally the same. That is the identity which is lost in speech, and forever lost when

God is named as God, when the name of God is actually spoken. To pronounce that name is to sanction, and finally to sanction, the loss of all identity which is eternally the same. Now that loss is a final loss, a finality evoked by the name of God, and with that loss all original identity is lost, and lost as an eternal and undifferentiated identity. Now every identity is other, and other in its actuality, other when it is spoken. So it is that the actual name of God, as opposed to an eternal or unspoken name of God, names otherness, and names a final otherness, an otherness that is finally other than itself.

Only an otherness that is finally other than itself can truly be other than an original and undifferentiated identity which is eternally the same. But only such an otherness can truly be the ground of a final otherness, an otherness which is so final that its sheer otherness precludes the possibility of its returning to an identity which is only itself. This final otherness is quite simply the world of actuality, a world which is actual in its otherness, and final in its actuality. We know the finality of actuality when we speak it, when we name God as God, for when we name God as God we name the finality of otherness, and thus we name an actuality which can never come to an end. Our naming of God seals the finality of actuality, of a final otherness, and that sealing makes manifest the finality of world, of our world, of the world of actuality. It is just because the naming of God makes manifest the finality of actuality that God can be named only when an original identity disappears. When that identity disappears then the name of God is spoken, and it is spoken when speech makes manifest its ground, and its ground in an otherness which is not and cannot be itself.

Who is that God who is manifest as God when we pronounce the divine name? Obviously the God who is manifest as God cannot be an unknown God. For the unknown is just that, unknown, or unnameable, whereas the manifest is present, and actually present in speech. But there it is an embodied presence, a presence in world. When the name of God is spoken, and spoken in actual speech, it makes manifest an actual identity, an identity which is intrinsically its own. An unknown God would be unspoken and unspeakable, and therefore not present, not actually present. For the actually present is speakable, even if it is unspoken, and it is speakable as actual, as that which is here. Therein it has an actual identity, a concrete and real identity, an identity which cannot pass into the unknown and the unsaid. So likewise the name of God has a concrete and real identity, an identity which cannot be unsaid, and it cannot be unsaid because it has actually been spoken, because its name has been pronounced.

Therefore when we speak the name of God we evoke a concrete identity, and an identity which cannot be unsaid, or not unsaid in speech. And that identity is otherness, a real and actual otherness, a final otherness which is even the otherness of itself. God is that otherness which is in exile from itself, an exile so actual that it is embodied in our speech, and an exile that becomes nameable as exile when we pronounce the name of God. Once that name has been pronounced, it cannot be unsaid. For the exile which that name evokes is a final exile, an exile that is and must be present wherever there is the possibility of speech. Speech speaks that exile, and it speaks it when it speaks, but only the name of God names that exile in its actuality, an actuality that is ultimate, and hence an actuality that can never cease to be itself. Indeed, the name of God makes manifest the finality of actuality, and makes it manifest by evoking an actual otherness which is ever the otherness of itself.

Only the naming of that otherness can make manifest the finality of exile, for once that otherness has been named, an identity can never appear, or be audible or speakable, which is simply and only itself. Simple identity perishes in actuality, for in actuality an actual here and an actual now are at hand, and not only are they at hand, they are overwhelming, so overwhelming that no other identity can be real or manifest in their presence. Eternal presence disappears in actuality, but it does not simply disappear, it reverses itself, becomes other than itself, and becomes other than itself in the advent of actual presence. Then speech speaks, for speech embodies the disappearance of eternal presence, and it does so by establishing an actual presence, a presence wherein omnipresence comes to an end. Presence becomes actual in speech, immediately actual, and so actual that all other presence perishes in the presence of speech. God is the name of the eternal perishing of eternal presence, and when speech speaks the name of God it sanctions itself as speech, it sanctions itself as a never-ending otherness, and therein makes manifest the once-and-for-all finality of speech.

Speech is that act which embodies a final otherness, and embodies it in a manifest identity, an identity wherein otherness is manifest as the otherness of itself. But otherness only becomes so manifest when the name of God is spoken, for only the utterance of that name evokes a final otherness, an otherness which is ultimately the otherness of itself. Nevertheless, that otherness is always present in speech, and present even when it is unuttered. For the act of speech embodies a pure otherness, an otherness which is in exile from itself. Speech is the self-embodiment of a final otherness, an otherness which is ever other than itself. Not only does that otherness speak in speech, it is the source of speech. Speech is the advent of that otherness, and not only its advent but its actualization, for otherness realizes itself in speech, it becomes itself or enacts itself by embodying itself as the otherness of itself. Apart from that embodiment otherness could not be itself, for then it would be unrealized and therefore unreal. But in that embodiment otherness is not only real, it is finally real, and real as the otherness of itself. That otherness which is the otherness of itself is quite simply an actual otherness, an embodied or realized otherness, an otherness which enacts itself. Speech is the self-enactment of otherness, the self-realization of otherness, it is that otherness which can only be itself.

But to speak of speech in such a manner as to evoke its necessity, its ultimate or final necessity, is to speak, even if only indirectly, of God. If God is the name of ultimate and final necessity, and of a necessity which can only be itself, which is to say an actual necessity, then God must be named as the ground of speech, and not only its ground, but its source as well. To speak of speech without speaking of God is to speak of a speech without an ultimate necessity, ground, or source. Such a speech could not be fully actual, or finally actual, and thus it might or might not continue to maintain its identity as speech. But this is precisely what we cannot say about speech. And we cannot say it not simply because we continue to speak, but also because we cannot speak without realizing actuality, an actuality whose presence cannot come to an end. Once we know that actuality, and we know it by speaking, and by listening, too, then we know the finality of speech, a finality that can neither be unsaid nor undone. When we know that speech cannot be unsaid, and actually know it, then we know a final or ultimate necessity, a necessity which speech itself has named as God.

But can we name God, can we actually pronounce that name? Finally, this is to ask if we can actually speak, if we can speak so as to call forth or embody an actual identity, an identity which is itself and no other. For we can evoke an actual or real identity only by embodying difference, a real and actual difference, a difference making identity manifest, and making it manifest as itself. Only the presence of difference calls identity forth, and it calls it forth in its difference from itself, in its difference from an identity which is eternally the same. Apart from the realization of difference, and its embodiment in speech, identity could be neither actual nor manifest. Yet difference is realized in speech, and there identity is manifest, but it is manifest only because of the presence of otherness, an otherness which becomes finally present in speech. Otherness speaks in speech, but when it speaks itself, and speaks only itself, it speaks the name of God. To ask whether we can name God is to ask whether we can speak of an inherent and intrinsic otherness, an otherness which is the origin and ground of speech.

How can we speak of a final otherness, and of the presence of a final otherness, without speaking of God? Yet if we can speak of God, can we address God, can we evoke His presence by pronouncing that name? This is to ask if the actual utterance of the name of God calls forth a presence that otherwise would not be at hand. Speech is act, and it remains act even when it is silent. But does it significantly differ from itself in terms of what it says? For speech does not simply differ from the unsaid, it differs from itself, and differs from itself as it speaks, a difference which is inseparable from the presence and the actuality of speech. Nevertheless, it is possible that neither the evocation nor the pronunciation of the divine name evokes an identity that differs as such from that difference which is present in all speech. If this were so it would be insignificant whether or not the name of God has ever actually been spoken, for if no truly unique identity is called forth by this name, and only called forth by its utterance, then the name of God would have no more consequence than any other name. But is it possible, and actually possible, either to recall or to speak an ultimate otherness without evoking the name of God? And if it is not possible, and not possible in speech itself, then surely the pronunciation of the name of God evokes a special presence, an all-too-special presence, a presence that can be called forth by no other act of speech.

Not only do we evoke a special presence when we speak the name of God, but we evoke it in ourselves, in our speech, a speech whose utterance openly and manifestly calls forth an otherness which is only itself, an otherness which is the other of itself. That otherness is not only addressed when we speak the name of God, it is present, and present in the very act of our saying God. Thus we address God when we actually pronounce that name, and we know that we address God, and inescapably know it, for the utterance of that name releases, or makes manifest, a final otherness which is evoked by no other name. That otherness speaks in our speech when we speak the name of God, thereby it addresses us in its presence, and addresses us in our act of speech. Not only does it address us, but it addresses us in its finality, and so much so that once we have been addressed by its presence we can never again recover a speech which is unaffected by that voice. And it is just because we bear the imprint of that voice, and bear it even in its seeming absence, that we know that voice as present.

Consequently, the voice of God is present, and is present as call, a call that calls forth an ultimate act, an act which is itself a response to the presence of a final otherness. It is the presence of that otherness which evokes an ultimate response, for its pure otherness assaults all identity that would only be itself, thereby bringing the isolation of all such identity to an end. The end of such isolation is realized in response, and finally realized, so much so that now identity can realize itself only by being other than itself, only by being other than the sameness of itself. Identity now enters into exile from itself, but it does so only by embodying the actuality of the otherness to which it responds. Then identity realizes itself in the act of response, an act releasing identity from the identity of itself, releasing identity from an identity which is only itself. Now identity is embodied, and embodied in act, an act embodying the actuality of otherness in itself.

Indeed, identity actualizes itself as act, and it does so by embodying the actuality of otherness in its act. Once identity is actualized in act that identity can never be canceled or annulled. It cannot be lost because it is embodied, finally embodied, so finally embodied that identity can never again be only itself. Yet it is just because it is imperishable that the actualization of identity embodies a final call. That call calls identity out of itself, and calls it finally out of itself by calling it into the otherness of itself, an otherness wherein identity is finally actual and real. But identity is finally realized, and finally realized in act, only by embodying the actuality of a final otherness, an otherness which is ineradicable in its presence. And it is ineradicable in its presence because it is ineradicable in its otherness, only a pure otherness can bring unrealized identity to an end. That end is realized in the act of response to the presence of a final otherness, and that act realizes act itself, and realizes it so that the actuality of act can never pass away.

God is that final otherness which calls all identity out of itself, and calls it out of itself by calling it into exile from itself, an exile wherein identity ceases to be only itself. Identity ceases to be itself in act, for in act identity is embodied, and embodied by passing into the otherness of itself. Now identity is itself only by being other than itself, for once identity is actualized in act it can never again be silent and unheard or solitary and alone. Act is embodiment, embodiment in world, and in act identity is embodied in the world of actuality. But act is embodiment only insofar as it is exile, an exile free from an unrealized and nonactual identity, and therefore an exile from an identity of silence, an exile from the identity of the unsaid. In that exile identity passes out of its sameness into otherness, into the otherness of actuality, and into the finality of act. God is the name of the ground of act, of its final ground; hence God's is the name of the necessity of act, a necessity that we both evoke and sanction when we pronounce the name of God.

To speak of God is finally to speak of speech itself, of its ground, and its final ground, in that pure otherness which calls every identity out of itself. God is the name of the final source of speech, the name of that source which impels speech to speak, a source whose very presence calls forth the act of speech. Yet to speak of God is not simply to speak of a ground or source, it is to evoke the presence of that source, to make manifest a ground which calls, and calls even now when its name is spoken. We name God when we speak His name, and we actually name Him, thereby evoking the actual presence of the final ground of speech, a presence which speaks when we pronounce the name of names. That presence speaks in our speech, and by speaking of God we embrace that presence and make it our own, and make it our own by pronouncing that name which evokes the ultimate necessity of speech. Simply to pronounce that name is not only to evoke the necessity of speech but to sanction it as well. Thereby speech sanctions its ground, and its sanctions it by naming it, by naming it as God.

In naming God we embody an ultimate call, therein that call is present, and it is present in speech. Once that call is spoken, otherness is finally embodied in speech, and exile becomes the manifest destiny of speech. But when speech speaks of God it does not thereby make manifest a blank and empty otherness. For speech names God in speaking of God, and naming makes manifest a concrete and actual identity. Moreover, in naming God speech simultaneously negates the namelessness of otherness and sanctions otherness in its pronunciation of the divine name. Not only does speech sanction a pure or final otherness in speaking of God, thereby it evokes that otherness as call, and embodies it as final call. Then otherness itself is manifest as call, and not only is it manifest as call but it speaks as call, and speaks as call when the name of God is uttered. Otherness speaks in our speech when we speak of God. Then the namelessness of otherness is negated and reversed by speech, and reversed by that speech which names final otherness as ultimate call. Once that call is spoken, otherness ceases to be simply other, for now otherness speaks in call, and it can speak only by ceasing to be simply and only other.

When we say God we say the unsayable, and when we name God we name the unnameable, but it is precisely thereby that we speak. Finally, speech itself says the unsayable and names the unnameable, for the unsaid is unsayable until it is said in speech. By speaking of God we make manifest the unsayability of speech itself, we say the unsayable and say the unsayable by saying God. But all speech says the unsayable. For namelessness is named in actual speech, and that naming reverses namelessness, and reverses it by naming it. By speaking of God we make manifest the ground of speech, and our naming of God makes this reversal manifest or audible. For our naming of God is manifestly a naming of final otherness, and in that naming we can hear the voice of otherness, the voice of a pure or final otherness. Yet when that otherness is spoken it ceases to be simply other if only because it speaks.

While otherness ceases to be simply other when it is spoken, it does not thereby cease to be other. Indeed, otherness is most other when it is spoken. For then it is an embodied otherness, an otherness which is actual and immediate. Moreover, it is most other by not being only other. Then its otherness can be present, and actually present, in speech. That presence sounds when the name of God is spoken, and it sounds by negating and reversing the silence of the merely other, a silence that is reversed, and finally reversed, when otherness speaks. Then otherness is manifest, and it is manifest by being spoken. But in being spoken it is sanctioned, for it can be spoken only by speaking the name of God. So it is that otherness is most actual in its otherness when the name of God is pronounced, that naming calls forth the full actuality of otherness, an actuality that now becomes audible as call. It is audible as call because it is spoken as call, and it can be spoken as call only by being totally actual. Only the fully actual is actually spoken, and the name of God can be actually spoken only in the presence of a final otherness which is totally actual and manifest. To speak the divine name is to embody that presence, and finally to embody it, for the utterance of that name marks the end of everything which is simply and only other.

We realize an end of otherness in speaking the name of God, for that naming embodies the end of all otherness which is merely other, and makes manifest an otherness so near that it is manifest as call. Now otherness is call, as the actuality of otherness is embodied in speech, a speech wherein otherness names itself when the name of God is spoken. That naming unnames every otherness which is not present or spoken here, and it unnames it by embodying it, for all otherness is embodied when the divine name is pronounced. But since otherness is now manifest or speakable only as call, and as ultimate call, then all otherness which is only otherness comes to an end, and comes to an end by becoming totally immediate and actual. Thus the naming of God is the sounding of a totally immediate otherness, and with that sounding speech sounds its own ground, and sounds it as that otherness which draws all otherness into itself. In this sounding all sound becomes manifest and audible, for the otherness of all sound is present here, and its presence calls forth everything which can respond to otherness, or everything which can hear and respond to speech.

Consequently, the presence of God in speech calls forth everything which can respond to otherness in its hearer, and in that response all identity is emptied of everything which is only itself. For in the presence of a pure and immediate otherness hearing can call forth from itself only that which is other than itself. Hearing becomes what it hears, and in hearing the sounding of otherness, and no other sound, it embodies that sound in itself, and wholly embodies it, so that the hearing of pure otherness now becomes identity itself. That hearing embodies an actual identity which can sustain and realize itself only by speaking a pure otherness. Then the speaking of that otherness becomes the realization of actual identity, and identity realizes itself by evoking and embodying the pure otherness of itself. Speech speaks that otherness when it speaks the name of God, and the hearing of that name actualizes an identity which can be itself only by being other than itself. Otherness is now totally present both in hearing and in speech, and in that presence the voice of otherness embodies the innermost and most actual identity of identity itself. Now otherness actually speaks, and when it speaks we hear: "I AM."

III

JUDGMENT

How can we listen, and listen to the actuality of speech, and hear, "I AM"? Now it is not possible simply to listen to speech, which is to say that it is not possible to be wholly passive in the presence of speech, for we can listen to speech only by way of response. When the name of God is uttered, a final and total otherness is evoked, and we can respond to that otherness only by embodying the actuality of otherness in our listening itself. Then we hear otherness, and hear it in its full actuality, but this hearing is possible, or is actual and real, only when we can hear otherness alone. However, to hear nothing but otherness is to lose all awareness of the same. Thereby a same which is only the same disappears or becomes inaudible, and inaudible in the hearing of pure otherness, a hearing in which otherness becomes fully embodied in the hearer. In that hearing the hearer becomes other than itself, and not only other than itself, but wholly other than itself. Then all real or integral identity passes into otherness, and only otherness, or pure otherness, is manifest or hearable as real identity. All identity is now fully actual as otherness, and to hear the voice of pure otherness is to hear, "I AM."

For to hear that voice, or to be in the presence of that otherness, is to lose all identity which is only itself. Thereby identity becomes other than itself, and is speakable or hearable only in its otherness, a pure otherness wherein identity itself is purely or wholly other. Only pure otherness can now say, "I AM," and "I AM" can only be heard as the voice of that otherness. Now identity is wholly in exile from itself and it can be manifest as identity only in its otherness from itself. Once this realization of a purely exiled identity has occurred, identity is grounded in the otherness of itself, and can act and be real as identity only insofar as it embodies and actualizes otherness. Otherness is not then alien to identity, it is its innermost center and ground, a ground without which identity would now be unrealized and unmanifest. Speech embodies this otherness, for speech can speak only when the speaker and the hearer are other than each other, and it is the act of speech which both establishes and realizes this otherness. Not only does speech establish the otherness of the speaker and the hearer, but it enacts that otherness in speech, and enacts it as a mutual otherness, an otherness wherein speech can speak only through the otherness of the hearer, and the hearer can hear only through the otherness of speech.

Now "I AM" is heard wherever voice speaks, for it sounds in the voice of speech itself, and its sounding negates every possibility of a self-enclosed identity within the horizon of its speech. Identity can now preserve itself in the sameness of its identity only by ceasing to listen. But this is impossible in the presence of speech, as its voice not only assaults all such identity, but assaults it so as to bring it to an end. This it does in call, for voice calls, and its calling calls every identity out of itself. Simply to be in the presence of call is to be called irresistibly, and so irresistibly that to hear call is to be called out of an isolated identity. All isolated presence ends when call sounds, and it ends with the enactment of call, an enactment which draws all presence out of itself. Then presence can be actual and real only insofar as it is directed to another, but it can be directed to another only insofar as it ceases to be itself, only insofar as it is called.

Calling embodies presence, and it embodies the presence of both speaker and hearer, so that the very hearing of calling is itself an act of self-negation. Once call is sounded, attention is present. But attention can be present only when the hearer attends, and attends to that which is other than itself. Attention is inseparable from that otherness to which it attends, an otherness established by the presence of call. That otherness calls attention to itself, and in calling attention to itself it realizes otherness in the hearer, so that the act of attention is an act embodying otherness. But attention is not only an embodiment of otherness, it is a self-embodiment of otherness. For attention itself enacts the otherness to which it attends, and enacts it in its own act of attention. So far from being a mere passivity, attention is fully act, and it is act without passivity, and without passivity because it attends and only attends. All passivity is negated in attention, and this negation is a self-negation, for attention enacts itself.

To hear "I AM," and to hear it in the voice of call, is to enact attention to the actual presence of pure otherness, a presence which thereby and only thereby becomes all-consuming. Now attention is a self-embodiment of pure otherness, and it can be present only through act, and only through its own act of self-negation. Such self-negation is truly act, and its own act, an act realizing a new identity of the hearer. The hearer who hears "I AM" in the voice of call does so only by way of the act of self-negation. But that act is truly the hearer's own, and so much so that it is only this act of self-negation which realizes the hearer's self-identity. Indeed, self-identity now becomes identical with self-negation. We could even say that identity only becomes manifest and actual as self-identity through the self-embodiment of pure otherness. Apart from the self-embodiment of otherness, identity could not stand out from itself, hence self-identity would then be neither manifest nor actual. Nor can self-identity appear and be real apart from identity's own embodiment of otherness. But when this self-embodiment is realized in identity's own act, an act establishing or realizing self-identity, then self-identity is identical with self-negation.

Now it is precisely the act of hearing "I AM," and hearing it in the voice of call, that realizes self-identity. Only thereby does identity realize itself as self-identity, for only thereby does identity embody pure otherness in itself. Not only does identity realize self-identity in hearing "I AM," but in hearing "I AM" as the voice of pure otherness, it can realize itself only as the reversal or otherness of "I AM." Self-identity is manifest and real only insofar as it is not, only insofar as it is not itself, or not an identity which is only itself. And it is just by not being itself that identity passes into self-identity. Only when identity becomes other than itself does it become manifest or actual as self-identity, for only thereby can identity pass beyond or transcend itself. Then if self-identity is understood as self-realization, it can be so understood only by apprehending self-realization as self-negation, a self-negation wherein identity loses and leaves behind all simple identity with itself.

Consequently, self-identity is the self-realization of the presence of pure otherness. In that realization, otherness ceases to be only other, and becomes instead the self-embodiment of otherness, an embodiment wherein otherness becomes the center and ground of actual presence. Now otherness realizes itself, and it realizes itself by knowing itself, by knowing its own identity. This occurs with the advent of self-identity, for self-identity is not simply the realization of otherness, it is the self-realization of otherness itself, a realization wherein otherness realizes itself. And it realizes itself by knowing itself, by knowing its own otherness as identity itself, an identity which now becomes manifest and actual as self-identity. When otherness realizes its own identity, and realizes it as self-identity, then self-negation is actually present, and not only actually present, but finally and irreversibly present. In that presence, self-negation is the ground of actual identity, and not only the ground, but the source of identity as well.

Once self-negation is the ground of actual identity, then identity can realize itself only by negating itself, and it can negate itself only by ever becoming other than itself. Therefore self-identity is a continual process of identity becoming its own other. This process is embodied in speech, and embodied in speech when speech makes manifest its ground. For not only does speech embody the ground of otherness, it embodies the ground of otherness in speech itself, and does so simply when it speaks. That ground speaks in speech itself, but when it speaks so as to make manifest its actual ground, it makes manifest a continual process of self-negation. This process is above all manifest when actual identity speaks, or when self-identity is manifestly present in speech. While all speech speaks only by continually embodying otherness, the voice of actual identity or self-identity makes that otherness manifest or audible, and audible in its pure otherness. And not only is it audible, it is audible as the source of speech, for speech names itself as otherness when it speaks so as to make its self-identity manifest.

Moreover, self-identity only becomes manifestly present in speech when speech embodies a pure otherness, and embodies that otherness in voice itself. Then the voice of speech negates itself when and as it speaks, it assaults itself simply in its presence as speech. For that presence is a self-negating presence, a presence that can be present only in its own otherness, and only in its own otherness to itself. That otherness, or the presence of that otherness to itself, impels a full and total response, a response in which identity continually negates itself, and negates itself so as to continue to act and be real. But that response is the realization of self-identity in speech, a realization wherein identity continually assaults itself, and assaults itself so that it can continue to speak. So it is that self-identity only becomes openly manifest in a purely negative speech, that is to say a speech which speaks only negation, and which speaks negation simply as speech.

A purely negative speech can quite simply be identified as

prophetic speech, and particularly so when prophetic speech is understood as comprehending all that speech which is directed to a total judgment, and which embodies that judgment in the actuality of speech itself. Then speech embodies a pure negativity within itself as speech. That negativity assaults everything within its reach, and assaults it insofar as it stands forth as a manifest or speakable identity, an identity which can be uttered or evoked by speech. To hear that speech is to undergo an ultimate shock, a shock which hurls its hearer out of all given or fixed identity, and places a final question upon the very possibility of identity itself. Prophetic speech releases that final question, and not only releases but embodies it, and embodies it in speech. Now speech embodies identity as question, and ultimate identity as ultimate question, a question which has only to be heard to be enacted, and whose enactment brings an end to the manifest ground of all actual identity.

While prophetic speech poses a final question, and poses it in its speech, the one thing that cannot be questioned in the presence of prophetic speech is the power and the presence of that speech itself. Genuine prophetic speech is self-authenticating, and a simple test of prophetic speech is whether or not its voice can be stilled by those who hear it, and stilled so as to annul or to dissolve the actuality of its speech. The call of genuine prophetic speech is irresistible, and irresistible to those who hear it, even if that hearing embodies an ultimate assault upon the hearer. And it does embody such an assault, and manifestly so, for its speech inverts and reverses every identity which it names or evokes. Nevertheless, hearing cannot evade its speech, and cannot evade it not simply because it is spoken, but rather because it is finally spoken, or spoken with a finality that hearing cannot challenge.

Of course, various degrees of prophetic speech are present in all actual embodiments of prophecy. But true prophetic speech is a purely negative speech, and it is present to the extent that it assaults and shocks its hearer. Accordingly, prophetic speech is addressed to the actuality of its hearer, and even if it embodies a power which transcends every particular actuality, its speech is nonetheless an actual speech, and it is directed to the full actuality of the occasion in which it is uttered. Within that actuality, the negativity of prophetic speech seeks out the fullest and most powerful expressions of identity in its midst, and names those identities with an undeniable finality. But that naming is a negative naming, for it names only to negate, and the actuality of its naming embodies the negativity of the named, a negativity which here strips the named of all sanctioned identity. Indeed, sanctioned identity is now first fully named, and thereby it is given a wholly negative identity. And only to the extent that such negative naming is actual and real is prophetic speech embodied.

Why does the listener listen to prophetic speech? No doubt a power is present here, even if it is a purely negative power, and that power elicits response. Not only does it elicit response, it actively calls for response, and does so in the sheer negativity of its assault, an assault which penetrates to the very center of all possible response. Those centers are called by the presence of prophetic speech, and called in such a manner that the call itself is irresistible, or irresistible to the extent that it is heard. But when it is heard, and as it is heard, response is both immediate and overwhelming, and so much so that here response reenacts the speech that it hears, and reenacts it so as to make it its own. Despite the fact that the negativity of prophetic speech so fully negates the identity of its hearer, that hearer responds at the center of its identity, and responds by reenacting this negation of its center. This it does not only by the itensity and immediacy of its response, but also by the manner and mode of its response, a response in which it resays or repeats the speech which it hears. That repetition occurs in speech itself, as prophetic speech impels its hearer to repeat its speech, and not to repeat it in rite or saga, but rather in the actuality of speech itself. Now, for the first time, the actuality of speech embodies the finality of ultimate act, and an act that can only be repeated or reenacted in the sounding of speech.

Hence the hearing of prophetic speech immediately issues in the resaying of that speech, a repetition in which the actuality of that speech is reenacted, and reenacted at and by the center of its hearer. This reenactment occurs in hearing itself, a hearing in which the hearer embodies what it hears, and embodies it in speech. Now listening becomes hearing, which is to say that listening passes into full and total attention, an attention in which listening becomes what it hears. Then speech is spoken even in being heard, and it is spoken in the sense that its full actuality passes into the hearer. Once this has occurred, and in and by its very occurrence, the hearer gains a new identity through its response, and an identity which is a full realization of the act of hearing. That act is now realized in its intention, and so realized that now hearing is purely act, an act in which actuality speaks, and in which it speaks in hearing.

Hearing hears itself when it is purely act, and it hears itself in speech, a speech which is its own. But it is not only its own, for it is a speech which has sounded, and has sounded in the voice of another, and not only in the voice but in the presence of another. Now that presence passes into hearing itself, and as it passes into hearing, hearing not only ceases to be present as a presence which is simply itself, it becomes a presence which is the otherness of itself. In that presence, hearing is itself only by being the otherness of itself. Now hearing speaks that otherness in its hearing, a hearing which is uniquely its own, and which is nevertheless a hearing of the pure otherness of the full actuality of speech. That otherness is now fully embodied in the hearer, and so much so that now hearing and speech are one. And they are one in the hearer, in the hearer which speaks when it hears, and fully speaks in the full realization of hearing.

Now hearing is speech and so likewise and simultaneously

is it hearing. Moreover, it is a negative speech and a negative hearing, a hearing and speech which are self-negating, and self-negating in their very presence as hearing and speech. Only a process of self-negation could unite hearing and speech, for each can pass into the other only by ceasing to be itself, only by ceasing to be a hearing which is only hearing and a speech which is only speech. Of course, hearing and speech pass into each other whenever and wherever speech sounds. But only when hearing is fully actualized as speech does hearing fully pass into speech. Then hearing speaks whenever it hears, and it fully speaks, but it can do so only by embodying a negation of itself, a self-negation in which it speaks by hearing. To speak by hearing, and fully to speak, is to embody self-negation at the center of hearing, at the center of that presence which hears. Here, self-negation is act, and fully act, an act which enacts itself. And it enacts itself by realizing itself, by realizing a new identity at the center of hearing. This identity is a double identity, an identity which hears and speaks at once, and which hears and speaks in a single and all-consuming act.

When identity is doubled, it is not only divided from itself, but it is united with itself by that very division. This union is manifest when hearing speaks, and it is manifest at the center of hearing, and above all manifest in the self-identity of that center. For that self-identity is a double identity, an identity which is doubled in its innermost center, and which realizes its own identity by a doubling of hearing and speaking into a single act. No alien identity is present here. Or, rather, the identity which is present is alien only insofar as it is alien to itself. Alien to itself it certainly is, for the doubling of identity is self-alienation. It is self-alienating because it doubles itself, and it doubles itself in its own act, an act which is integral to its own identity. That identity is not simply a double identity, it is an identity which doubles itself, and doubles itself when it is most fully and actually itself.

Identity is fully realized in act only by being released from itself. That release embodies identity in act, but identity is embodied in act only when it ceases to be simply and only itself. Yet only when identity is doubled does identity release itself into the fullness of act. Thereby identity enacts its own release from that identity which is only itself and no more. That enactment hurls identity out of itself, thereby identity is in exile from itself, and only by being in exile from itself can identity release or realize itself in act. The doubling of identity is identity's own realization of itself in act, a realization whereby identity propels itself, and propels itself out of itself and into act. Now the exile of identity from itself, and its consequent embodiment in act, is identity's own self-embodiment in act. This occurs only when identity is alienated from itself, or is in exile from itself, a self-exile which is self-alienation, and a self-alienation which realizes identity itself.

Self-identity, too, is itself in self-alienation, for it is in self-alienation that identity is most actually other, and it is the actuality of otherness which releases and realizes self-identity. That actuality also releases identity's embodiment in act, an embodiment which is possible only when identity is other than itself, and which is fully possible only when identity itself is the source of its own otherness. These possibilities become actual in self-alienation, as the self-doubling of self-alienation realizes an identity which is itself the source of its own otherness. That identity is self-identity, or the full realization of self-identity, a realization which is only realized in act. But it is realized in act only because the doubling of identity forcloses the possibility of identity's simply being itself. Only the alienation of identity from itself establishes the full possibility of act, an act which is identity's own, for only thereby does it become impossible for identity to be simply and only itself.

Now identity is called, and it is called to act, and to act in the actuality of otherness, an otherness in which all given or manifest identity comes to an end. And it comes to an end in act itself, it ends as act fully releases or realizes itself, for act only acts by enacting the otherness of identity itself. That enactment is embodied in act, and its embodiment embodies identity, and embodies identity so that the otherness of identity is identity itself. Thereby identity is not only called to act, it is called in act, and called out of itself in the realization of act. This occurs wherever act is embodied, and it occurs to the extent that act is embodied, as the realization of act actualizes the otherness of identity, and actualizes it by establishing it in the immediacy of presence. In act, immediacy is present, and it is present to the degree that act is act, as act releases immediacy, and releases it in the actuality of otherness.

When identity is so called out of itself, thereby embodying call in act, it realizes a new identity of itself, and realizes that identify only by losing all identity which is not embodied in its act. Here, identity is act and it is identity only insofar as it is act. So it is that it is only the loss of an identity which is only identity which embodies act, and that loss not only is act but it impels act, for the loss of identity is identical with the embodiment of call. When that loss is actual, and immediately actual, loss passes into act, a pure act free of all disembodied identity. That act calls all identity in its presence, and calls it to its presence, an actual and immediate presence wherein pure identity is act and only act. Simply to be in the presence of an act which is only act is to be called out of all disembodied identity, and not only to be called but to be finally called, as call now brings an end to the speakable and hearable ground of all that identity which is only itself.

Once call has sounded in act, and has become embodied in act, a speech which fails to embody call becomes impossible in its presence. Then hearing hears nothing of that which was once manifest, for there is nothing there to be heard, nothing actually there. One can listen for the presence of the absent, but one cannot hear it, for hearing can hear only what is actually present. But if nothing is actually present then hearing cannot hear. Once listening has passed into hearing, as it does in the presence of call, then listening can no longer simply listen, and instead can listen only insofar as it hears. The voice of call, or the call of call, in its pure immediacy, ends all hearing which hears anything other than call, anything truly other than call. Then, and only then, hearing is fully established, and is established as a hearing which only hears. Such pure hearing hears nothing of that which fails to embody call, hence it cannot hear a speech which does not call, and all such speech becomes inaudible for a hearing that hears and only hears.

Pure hearing calls the hearer out of listening, and out of listening into act, an act that is a response to call. Thus act is a response to the presence of call, and it acts by embodying call. But act can embody call only by disembodying its hearer from all hearing which does not hear call. This occurs in judgment, in final judgment, a judgment which brings all listening to an end. Listening comes to an end in judgment because judgment is the actualization of call, and the actualization of call embodies call in the immediacy of hearing. That immediacy is a pure immediacy, an immediacy which only hears, and which only hears call. Listening perishes in that immediacy because listening can listen to whatever sounds or might sound. But listening cannot listen when judgment occurs because judgment draws all presence into itself. Then listening can no longer listen because judgment, pure judgment, commands all attention to itself. Only hearing is possible in the presence of judgment, and that hearing hears call as command.

Call speaks in pure hearing, and it speaks as command. But call can speak as command only when judgment has ended all identity which cannot respond to call. So it is that call only speaks as command when hearing is present, a pure hearing which only hears call, for only that hearing responds to call in act. Accordingly, command is truly present only in obedience, for only obedience enacts command, and command is not present if it is not enacted. In no sense may command, or the command of call, be construed as an imperative, for this would be to misconstrue the voice of call. The command of call is present, and immediately present in voice, a voice whose sounding hearing hears, and hears because its is a commanding presence. But the presence of the voice of call, and its immediate presence, forecloses the possibility of a command which is distant and apart. So likewise there is no possibility here of a command which is simply and only a command. Here it is call which speaks as command, and it speaks only insofar as it is present.

Not only does command speak only insofar as it is present, but it is present only insofar as it is heard, and it is heard only in response. Call speaks only in response, and only in response to its presence as command, a presence which can be truly present only in obedience. If the command of call can be present only in response, then here command is not a commandment, for it is not a command which simply commands, just as it is not a command which can be separated from obedience. In the same manner, an obedience which is a true obedience to the command of call is not a simple or a passive obedience. It obeys by embodying call, and by embodying call in act, an embodiment which is an immediate response to the pure voice of call. If command is not embodied, then it is not heard, or not truly heard, and then it cannot be commanded, or not commanded as the command of call. True command has only to be heard to be embodied, and it is embodied to the extent that it is heard.

But command can be heard, or truly heard, only in pure hearing, and that hearing is possible only in the presence, and the immediate presence, of judgment. Judgment embodies a negation of everything which stands apart from the voice of call, and it is precisely the enactment of that negation which makes command possible, and command can be heard only insofar as that negation is present and actual. That negation is actual in the hearer, and is present in the hearer to the extent that the hearer hears. Finally, hearing is an actualization of negation, for it is the realization of the end of listening, the end of listening to what is not fully and actually said. When that listening ends, then hearing truly hears, and it hears only what is said. Pure attention is then given only to the voice of speech, and only to the present and actual voice of speech. Yet such attention is possible only when no attention is given to any other presence or possible presence, as attention now becomes a commanding attention, an attention which allows no other attention in its presence. Thus it is a total attention, and it is possible only insofar as the hearer hears only the actuality of voice, an actuality which can be fully present only when nothing else is heard.

Nothing else is heard in pure hearing, for that hearing is incapable of listening and thus it hears only voice. And the voice it hears is the voice of call, for voice can be fully present only as call, or only as call to those who hear. Now not only does call speak as command, but it speaks as command only to those who hear. But to those who hear, voice is command, and it is present to the extent that voice speaks. Voice itself can now be heard only when listening is absent. For now voice speaks as voice itself, and in its presence listening passes into hearing. Voice calls as that occurs, and it calls to the extent that it occurs. But it can call only in the actualization of negation in the hearer, only in the realization of the end of the listener. Pure voice speaks only to self-negation, and only as self-negation. That self-negation is pure act, and it is the act of the hearer, and the act of the hearer in responding to call. Now command is obeyed, and it is obeyed not as as external or alien commandment, but rather as a voice which can only be heard, and only be heard in self-negation.

Hearing is judgment, and pure hearing is pure judgment, for it negates everything which cannot be heard, and everything which cannot be heard in the actual presence of voice. Such hearing is also a saying, for it says what it hears, and says it by embodying it in act. That act is one of pure negation, and of active and actual negation. Above all it is an act of self-negation, and here all negation proceeds out of self-negation, for all negation issues out of the hearer's response to call. That response is possible only insofar as the hearer can hear nothing but call, and the possibility of hearing nothing but call can be realized only when the hearer itself has enacted a negation of the unhearable, and enacted it in itself as hearer. This enactment can occur only at the center of hearing, for only there is hearing most fully and most actually itself. Yet when the hearer enacts a negation of the unhearable at its own center it enacts a negation of itself. For it is precisely the unhearable which is the center of every identity which has not come under judgment.

Judgment negates the unhearable, and it negates the unhearable as that which cannot be heard, and as that which cannot be heard at the center of hearing. Thus judgment is manifest to the hearer as self-judgment, and is actual as self-judgment as well, a self-judgment wherein the center of identity hears itself, and hears itself as that which is fully hearable. Hearing speaks in self-judgment, and it speaks by negating itself, by negating itself as unhearable. Then self-identity stands naked and alone, naked inasmuch as it is stripped of the cloak of silence, and alone inasmuch as it is present only in hearing. Now hearing hears even silence as speech, for silence has become speakable, and not only speakable but actually spoken in self-judgment. For self-judgment ends the silence of self-identity, and ends it by ending listening, bringing that listening to an end which listens to the silence of itself. The silence of the listener becomes speakable in self-judgment, and it speaks by ending as silence, or by ending as a silence which cannot be heard. Thereby the listener is naked to itself, and naked to itself because it hears itself, and hears itself as that which is nothing but the hearable.

So likewise the listener now stands alone, and stands alone in hearing, a hearing in which only the hearer hears. Listening can embody a mutual presence, a presence of multiple listeners, and a presence wherein listeners can listen with each other. But the passivity of listening ends in hearing, and it ends because hearing is act, and not only is it act but in its purity it is pure act, an act which wholly enacts itself. This enactment occurs in self-judgment, for self-judgment judges itself, and in its fullness it wholly judges itself. There is nothing present in the fullness of self-judgment but the act of judgment itself, that act is here and wholly here, and so much so that the hearer can hear its presence nowhere else. Consequently, the hearer stands alone in self-judgment. Indeed, it is self-judgment, and self-judgment alone, which fully realizes solitude, a solitude which is the embodiment of a solitary act. Only self-judgment is a truly solitary act for it is self-judgment alone which is act and actor at once, an act which enacts itself. And self-judgment enacts itself whenever and wherever it is possible, which is to say that self-judgment occurs wherever solitude is present, and it occurs whenever act enacts itself. But it is just this enactment, and this enactment alone, which realizes the fullness of self-identity.

Now self-identity stands alone, and it stands alone in its act, the act of self-judgment. Once this act has occurred, and has been realized in its hearer, then the hearer has embodied final judgment, and has embodied it in itself as hearer. Then the act of judgment is all-consuming, and it is heard and enacted wherever and whenever the hearer hears. So it is that the hearer that hears a judgment that is wholly here hears judgment everywhere, and hears it everywhere because it hears judgment alone, it hears judgment wherever it hears. When judgment is wholly here its hearer hears its presence nowhere else, but nevertheless it hears presence itself as judgment, and therefore it hears judgment wherever there is presence. Nothing whatsoever stands outside of this presence, or nothing which can be heard, as presence itself now becomes identical with judgment. But such presence is manifest as judgment only to self-identity, and is actual as judgment only in self-identity, as self-identity, and self-identity alone, fully embodies judgment.

Accordingly, self-identity is identical with self-judgment, and the fullness of self-identity is identical with the fullness of self-judgment. Self-identity can stand as self-identity only insofar as it judges, and only insofar as it judges itself. But can self-identity then stand, and stand as itself? This is to ask if it can hear, hear and only hear, hear and only hear itself. Of course, self-identity does not simply hear itself, and this is not only because it does not simply hear, but also because it hears the voice of call, and hears that voice in judgment itself. But that voice is now fully manifest and actual in self-judgment, and in self-judgment alone, for self-judgment fully embodies voice, and fully embodies voice because it fully hears. When voice is so present, so fully present, it is present as self-judgment, but nevertheless it is fully present as voice. Now voice is call which calls its hearer to self-judgment. But that voice is truly call, and it truly calls by calling as self-judgment. That call fully releases identity, and it releases identity as self-identity, a self-identity which is self-judgment. Self-identity is realized by judgment, and it realizes itself by self-judgment, but that self-judgment is itself the gift or grace of call.

The gift or grace of call is the saying of "I AM," a saying which is heard in judgment, and which is heard by being said, and said again, in self-judgment. Self-judgment is a resaying of "I AM," a repetition of "I AM" in hearing, and a repetition which says "I AM" by enacting it in hearing. Such hearing reverses the manifest identity of "I AM," and it reverses it by hearing it. For hearing is the embodiment of the otherness of speech. But speech is truly present in hearing, and it truly speaks when hearing fully hears, for hearing only hears the actuality of the said. Hearing resays the actuality of "I AM" by enacting it as self-judgment, therein the actuality of "I AM" passes into hearing, and identity fully realizes its identity as self-identity. Self-identity stands, and stands alone, and stands as itself, only by resaying the command of "I AM" in the obedience of hearing, only by the repetition of the voice of "I AM" in the finality of self-judgment. Self-identity is actual and real only insofar as self-judgment is actual and real, and self-judgment is actual only insofar as it actually says "I AM," and says it by resaying it as self-judgment. Hence the repetition of "I AM" is the actualization of self-negation, and the actualization of self-negation in self-identity.

IV

INCARNATION

Voice speaks. And when it speaks, and as it speaks, it embodies itself. Speech is the embodiment of voice, and that embodiment is the act of voice itself. Therefore speech is also the enactment of voice, the self-enactment of voice, it is that act wherein voice enacts itself. Only voice is act and self-identity at once, and is self-identity in its act of speech, an act which is necessarily individual and unique. Voice is that act, and that act alone, which is ever other than every other act, and is other, and truly other, solely because it is itself. Therefore voice is otherness itself, and is otherness in its own identity, in its own act. This otherness is fully and truly its own, and is its own because voice acts; it speaks. Speech is the self-identity of voice. But as speech, voice is other than itself, and is other than itself precisely because it speaks.

Yet voice is not simply other than itself, and this because it is not passively other than itself. Voice enacts its otherness from itself, and embodies that otherness in its own speech. Consequently, voice is the actualization of self-negation. The identity of voice is only its own, but it is its own only because voice as voice is other than its own. The ownness of voice, its integral and individual identity, resides in its otherness from itself. Only that otherness is the arena of voice, and it is an arena which is voice's own, for it is the otherness of voice itself. Voice enacts itself only by negating itself, and it embodies itself only by embodying the otherness of itself, an otherness which is truly and only its own. When voice speaks it is only itself, yet it is itself only by being other than itself. Thus voice as voice is pure act, an act which embodies itself, and embodies itself by enacting the otherness of itself. Pure act truly enacts itself, and it fully and wholly enacts itself, but it enacts itself by negating itself.

When "I AM" speaks, it speaks as voice, and as voice which is truly itself. But speech is truly speech only insofar as it is heard, and the voice of "I AM" is truly voice only insofar as it is embodied and enacted. That occurs in hearing, and when hearing repeats and re-presents the voice of "I AM, "I AM" speaks in the act of hearing itself. Yet "I AM" speaks only insofar as it is heard, and it speaks to the extent that it is heard. Thus the voice of "I AM" is not heard immediately, or not heard in its fullness and purity immediately or at once. That can occur only in the purity of hearing, only when hearing is pure act. But hearing, too, only becomes pure hearing when it fully negates itself, when it becomes wholly other than itself. This it does only insofar as speech is embodied and enacted in hearing, or only insofar as speech becomes hearing and hearing becomes speech. But to the extent that this occurs, and insofar as it does occur, hearing and speech pass into each other, and speech is hearing only insofar as hearing is speech.

Hearing can become speech only insofar as it negates itself as hearing, even if such negation is the purest act of hearing itself. And hearing does negate itself when it hears, for when and as it hears, and truly hears, it passes ever more fully into speech. But hearing speaks only by transcending and moving beyond itself as hearing, only insofar as its own act of hearing becomes other than itself. This is precisely the essence of pure act. For act is pure, or is pure act, only by passing beyond itself, only by becoming other than itself in its own act. Yet if hearing becomes speech in the fullness of its hearing, then so likewise does speech become hearing in that very act. If speech is truly speech only insofar as it is heard, then the realization of speech as speech occurs in hearing, and occurs in that hearing which is pure act. Speech realizes itself by transcending itself, but it transcends itself by actualizing itself in that hearing which is speech. Then speech speaks by hearing, and by hearing itself. But speech can hear itself only by being other than itself, even if in that otherness it truly realizes itself as speech.

Speech actualizes itself in self-negation, and this actualization of self-negation embodies itself in voice. Voice realizes the self-identity of speech, and this identity is enacted and embodied in self-negation, in identity's negation of itself. Thus the identity of "I AM" is only realized as self-identity through the self-negation of "I AM." When "I AM" is heard, and is heard as "I AM," it realizes its self-identity, its own identity as "I AM." Therein the voice of "I AM" passes into hearing, and the hearing of the voice of "I AM" becomes the speech of "I AM" itself. This occurs through the simultaneous self-negation of hearing and speech. For hearing negates itself as hearing to realize itself as speech, and speech negates itself as speech to realize itself as hearing. Each movement is not only a movement of self-negation, but also a movement of transcendence. Not only does hearing transcend itself in becoming speech, but so likewise does speech transcend itself in becoming hearing.

Only in hearing does speech realize its self-identity, and only therein does it realize itself as act. Hearing embodies speech, and it enacts it as well, and it is precisely thereby that speech truly becomes itself. Accordingly, the repetition of speech in hearing is the act of speech itself. Speech enacts itself in hearing, and it enacts itself to the extent that it is heard. Obviously speech is not always heard, or not fully heard, for speech must struggle to realize itself. So likewise the hearer must struggle to hear speech, must struggle to hear its source and ground, or to hear its speaker. Such struggle is truly a labor of the negative, for hearing can hear the speaker only by not hearing itself, only by negating itself. Yet it is also true that the speaker can be heard only insofar as its speech moves out of itself, only insofar as its speech is not its own, or not only its own. Indeed, it is just to the extent that its speech is not only its own that it is truly speech. Speech realizes itself as speech only to the extent that it negates and transcends its speaker. For only thereby is speech heard, and only thereby is it truly speech.

Speech empties its speaker, and empties its speaker insofar as it is heard, insofar as it is enacted and embodied. So it is that hearing is wounding, and it wounds not only the hearer but the speaker as well. For the speaker is wounded in the loss of its speech, the loss of its voice, the loss of its self-identity. True, the speaker fully realizes its identity, its self-identity, only through this loss of itself. But it gains itself only by losing itself, it becomes itself only by becoming other than itself. This occurs only as it struggles against itself, only as it empties itself of its identity as speaker. For the speaker who is speaker and only speaker stands alone and apart, and inasmuch as the speaker stands alone its voice cannot be heard. When voice is heard, it ceases to be alone and apart, and therein it ceases to be only voice. Voice then ceases to be the voice of its speaker, or of its speaker alone, and perishes as voice which is only itself. This occurs in hearing, in the hearing of voice, as voice in hearing becomes other than itself. Thereby the speaker loses its voice, or loses that voice which is only its own, and it is just this loss of voice which is realized when the speaker is heard.

Voice speaks, yes, and in truly speaking it is heard. Thereby voice ceases to be only itself, and perishes in its identity as voice and voice alone. But it is just this perishing which realizes the self-identity of voice. Apart from its end as a voice which is only voice, voice could not speak, or it could not speak so as to be heard. The hearing of voice ends the solitude of voice, and voice ceases to be alone and apart to the extent that it is heard. But only thereby does voice truly becomes itself, does it truly speak. Speech realizes the self-identity of voice, and realizes it by bringing voice's identity as voice and voice alone to an end. That end occurs in hearing, and only in hearing does voice realize its self-identity. Voice, however, does not simply perish in hearing. It far rather transcends itself, and it transcends itself by ceasing to be voice alone, by ceasing to be alone and apart as a voice which is only voice. When voice passes into hearing, it not only ceases to be itself, or ceases to be only itself, it is precisely thereby that it fully realizes itself, that it realizes its own self-identity. For it is in hearing, and in hearing alone, that voice becomes pure act.

Voice enacts itself in hearing, and it enacts itself by embodying itself, by embodying itself in hearing. Then hearing becomes pure hearing, and it becomes pure hearing by wholly embodying voice. Hearing is voice, is voice which realizes itself, and realizes itself in the act of hearing. When hearing realizes itself as pure hearing, or passes into pure hearing, it thereby embodies voice. But hearing's embodiment of voice is also and simultaneously voice's embodiment of itself. For voice itself speaks in hearing just as hearing speaks when it fully hears. And the speech of hearing is the voice of speech, is the voice of that speech which is fully actual and real. Speech is fully real or realized only in hearing, and it is only in hearing that voice knows or realizes itself. Consequently, voice realizes its self-identity in hearing and in hearing alone. So likewise the purity of voice is solely realized in the purity of hearing, the pure act of voice is simultaneously the pure act of hearing. Speech and hearing are identical when each is fully itself, and it is the identity of voice and hearing which is realized when each fully realizes itself.

Thus the voice of "I AM," simply because it is voice, not only becomes other than itself when it is heard, but also is identical with itself in that very hearing. But it is identical with itself, and actually identical with itself, only insofar as it is other than itself. In no sense may an actual identity be confused with a simple identity. Simple identity is simply itself, and it is itself apart from act or enactment. Act ends simple identity, and it ends it because it is act. Once act has occurred, or has been enacted, a simple or undifferentiated identity is no more. Enacted identity is other than itself, and other than itself because it is actual, because it acts. Accordingly, identity is other than itself when it is actual or real, and other than itself because it stands out from itself, and stands out and apart from itself by virtue of its act or enactment. "I AM" as a simple or undifferentiated identity is simply and only itself. That identity ends when "I AM" speaks, and it ends simply because "I AM" speaks. "I AM" enacts its own otherness from itself in its act, in its act of speech. That act is the voice of "I AM," and this voice is the actual identity of "I AM," an identity realized, and only realized, by the act or enactment of "I AM" itself.

But that act is the otherness of "I AM," an otherness which is heard by "I AM" itself, and heard as the voice of "I AM" passes into hearing. If voice is the actual identity of "I AM," that identity becomes self-identity insofar as it is heard. And it is heard to the extent that it is spoken, to the extent that it is fully and wholly spoken. Yet this can occur, and does occur, only to the extent that the actual identity of "I AM" becomes ever other than the simple or undifferentiated or original identity of "I AM." Thus the hearing of "I AM" ends the original identity of "I AM," an ending which is the inevitable consummation of "I AM's" own act of speech. Indeed, the actualization of "I AM" is identical with the ending of the original identity of "I AM." Only with and in that ending does "I AM" realize its self-identity, a self-identity which is actual in its voice. Not only does "I AM" realize itself in its voice, but it knows itself in its voice, and knows itself by hearing itself, by hearing its voice as its own.

The voice of "I AM," the actual identity of "I AM," is the embodiment of "I AM." And the embodiment of "I AM" is the hearing of "I AM," a hearing wherein "I AM" is identical with itself even in its otherness from itself. Embodiment is act, and act is self-negation, the self-negation of an original or undifferentiated identity. Therefore embodiment is emptying, and not only emptying but self-emptying, the self-emptying of original identity. Identity empties itself in its embodiment, and it is precisely thereby, and only thereby, that identity actualizes or realizes itself. "I AM" actualizes and realizes itself in its voice, but only the hearing or the embodiment of its voice is the self-realization of "I AM." That occurs wherever identity undergoes self-negation, or wherever identity is self-emptied or embodied. But it only fully occurs in pure or total self-emptying, and only therein does the ground of all actual identity fully realize and actualize its own self-identity. That self-identity is the self-realization of its ground and source, the self-actualization of an original "I AM."

The self-realization of "I AM" is not a simple or immediate act, not an act occurring immediately or at once. For it realizes itself in an actual process of realization, a process wherein it continually enacts itself. This occurs in the voice of "I AM," a voice which is actual, and a voice which is actual because it is heard. Not only is it heard, it is heard again and again, and heard continually as it continues to speak. Voice is always heard, even if its is only heard by its speaker, and it is also always heard by another, even if that other is the otherness of its speaker. Hearing is the embodiment of voice, and it embodies voice in the otherness of voice. That otherness is hearing, for hearing is the actual otherness of voice, and it is in that otherness that voice realizes itself. But it can realize itself only in the actuality of otherness, and in the actuality of its own otherness, an actuality which is truly the otherness of itself. Hence voice, or the actuality of voice, is and must be heard by another, an other than itself.

It is in that hearing that voice embodies itself, and embodies itself by realizing itself in and as the otherness of itself.

Yet voice can realize itself as the otherness of itself only by emptying itself of its original identity. This is just what occurs in the self-actualization of voice, a process of self-realization wherein the original identity of voice becomes ever other than itself. And it becomes ever other than itself by becoming ever more fully and finally embodied and enacted. That embodiment and enactment occurs not simply in the hearing of voice, but rather in that hearing, and that hearing alone, wherein voice fully passes into hearing. Then voice ceases to be voice. But it is just this ending of voice which is the actualization of voice itself. This actualization occurs continually, and it occurs again and again in concrete acts, in concrete acts of hearing. Such hearing is immediate, and it not only occurs immediately, but it occurs in immediate acts. These acts assault the hearer, and they assault the hearer with the immediate power of voice. That power is fully present when voice is heard, and it is totally present in pure hearing. Therein voice not only passes into hearing, but it releases itself in its pure immediacy, an immediacy which is both the emptying and the transcendence of pure voice.

The pure emptying of voice is the pure transcendence of voice, a transcendence which is self-transcendence, for it is the self-enactment and the self-embodiment of voice. When the voice of "I AM" realizes itself as pure transcendence, it fully empties itself of its original voice and identity. That emptying is the self-embodiment of the voice of "I AM," a self-embodiment which is a self-transcendence of the original identity of "I AM." Now the voice of "I AM" is a wholly self-actualized immediacy, and an immediacy wherein voice is totally present in hearing. But this presence, this self-actualizing presence, is a self-negating presence. Only the self-negation of the original presence of the voice of "I AM" can realize that presence in the immediate actuality of hearing. Pure hearing is the total embodiment of voice, an embodiment wherein voice is the otherness of itself. That otherness is the pure otherness of the original presence of "I AM." Therefore, in that otherness, the original identity of "I AM" realizes itself as "I AM NOT."

If "I AM" is the original identity of the voice of "I AM," then only "I AM NOT" can be the fully embodied identity of the voice of "I AM." Not until the fullness of the original voice and identity of "I AM" has passed into the actuality and immediacy of pure hearing can "I AM" fully realize its self-identity. That identity is a fully embodied identity, a fully self-actualized identity, wherein "I AM" is wholly other than itself. And its otherness from itself is its self-enactment, its self-embodiment, its self-identity. Such otherness is heard in the full immediacy of hearing, but it is only fully heard in the pure immediacy of pure hearing. When hearing is pure, is pure act, it is wholly open to voice. That openness is the act of hearing itself, an act which is realized only in the hearing of voice, and in the hearing of that voice which is itself realized in this act. That realization is not only the self-realization of "I AM," it is the full actualization of the self-enactment of "I AM," a self-enactment which is the actualization of the self-emptying of "I AM." Therefore only "I AM NOT" can be the full actualization of "I AM," the full realization of the self-embodiment or self-actualization of "I AM."

Now it is just this passage from the positive to the negative, from "I AM" to "I AM NOT," which is the act of self-embodiment. This act is truly act, and pure act as well, and as pure act it is a movement of self-negation or self-emptying. But it is precisely thereby that identity is fully self-enacted or self-actualized. Only thereby does identity become fully actual and real as self-identity. For self-identity, or actual self-identity, is an embodied identity. Only insofar as identity actualizes and passes into its own otherness does it realize its self-identity. Only by becoming its own otherness does identity become itself, does it realize or enact itself. Accordingly, self-identity is not given, it is not immediately present or at hand. Self-identity is actual and real only insofar as it is realized and enacted, only insofar as it embodies itself in self-realization and self-enactment. That occurs only as identity becomes other than itself, and becomes ever other than itself, a process of self-realization culminating in identity's becoming wholly other than itself. Only an identity that is wholly other than itself can be a fully embodied identity. For only an identity that is wholly other than itself can be wholly actual and real, can be fully actualized and realized as self-identity. Then identity as self-identity is immediately present and at hand: "The time is fulfilled, and the Kingdom of God is at hand."

When self-identity has so realized itself, it has wholly embodied itself in actuality. Then the process or movement of self-negation becomes fully realized in actuality, and actuality itself becomes the self-identity of "I AM." But it is so only insofar as actuality is pure actuality, is pure immediacy, an immediacy wherein actuality wholly negates and empties itself. And this it does to the extent that actuality is the self-embodiment of the voice of "I AM." In that embodiment, "the Kingdom of God is at hand," and actually at hand, at hand in actuality. Yet it is so only insofar as it is the reversal or otherness of the original voice and identity of "I AM." Only in that reversal is "I AM" fully or purely actual, and only in that otherness is the voice of "I AM" fully embodied and enacted. Then it fully enacts itself as the otherness of itself, and in that self-enactment "I AM" is simultaneously wholly other than itself and the full realization of itself. For the self-realization of "I AM" is the self-embodiment of "I AM," an embodiment not only in actuality, but an embodiment as actuality as well.

Indeed, an actual embodiment, insofar as it is fully actual, can only be an embodiment as actuality. That actuality is itself the hearing of the voice of "I AM," a hearing embodying that voice in act. Now the "Kingdom of God" is at hand in act, in the act of hearing, and in that hearing which is pure hearing or pure act. As pure act, such hearing is wholly enacted, and it is wholly enacted in the fullness of act. That fullness of act is the self-enactment of "I AM," its self-embodiment as actuality. Therein the voice, and the whole voice, of "I AM" is released in act, and released in those acts which are the fullness of act itself. These acts can only be concrete acts, concrete and actual acts, acts which fully actualize act itself. Hearing, or pure hearing, is these acts, for pure hearing is act itself. That act is enacted in actual acts, in concrete acts which speak and embody the self-identity of "I AM." This self-identity can only be the "Kingdom of God" which is at hand in act, and not simply in act but in acts, in those acts which embody both the fullness and the purity of self-emptying or self-negation.

When the "Kingdom of God" is so at hand, it is present in its act, and present in those acts which embody pure hearing or pure act. These acts are the actualization of self-emptying or self-negation. And their presence, or their enactment, embody self-negation in actuality, in that actuality which is immediate and at hand. Then the realization of that actuality is the realization of self-negation or self-emptying. Now this occurs whenever act is fully enacted, whenever "time is full-filled." The fullness of time is the fullness of act, the fullness of pure act or actuality. Such fullness can only be the fullness of self-negation, as self-negation or self-empty-ing now becomes the innermost identity of actuality. This innermost identity of actuality is the identity of an actuality which itself is individual and unique. And it is necessarily individual and unique, for its identity is the consequence, and the real or realized consequence, of a unique and individual movement of self-negation. That movement or process is the self-negation or self-emptying of the original voice and iden-tity of "I AM." Once this movement has been fulfilled, as it is when the "Kingdom of God" is at hand, then it can be actual only as the reversal or otherness of the initial or primal identity of "I AM."

Now this otherness of "I AM," an otherness realized by

the self-emptying of "I AM," is not simply a real or actual otherness. For it is that otherness, and that otherness alone, which embodies in its own actuality a reversal of the primal identity of "I AM." If the primal identity of "I AM" is manifest and speakable as the ground and source of all actual otherness, then an actuality embodying its reversal can only be manifest and hearable as a self-negating otherness. Moreover, as a self-negating otherness its actuality can be heard only insofar as it is enacted and embodied in self-emptying. Such self-emptying is both an actual self-emptying and a self-emptying in actuality. On the one hand, it can occur only in concrete and actual acts, and on the other hand, it can be realized only in the full immediacy of actuality. Here, self-emptying is the self-negation of a real and actual identity. For it is the self-negation of the primal identity of "I AM," the self-emptying of the ground and source of actual otherness. That emptying can occur only in the self-identity, and the actual self-identity, of the self-emobidment of "I AM." Only in that actual self-identity can self-emptying be both fully actual and a full realization of actuality.

Then self-emptying is both full and final, and full and final in its actuality. In occurring in the self-embodiment of "I AM," and as the self-embodiment of "I AM," it must necessarily be a full realization of self-negation. For anything less than a full realization of self-negation could not be a self-embodiment of the ground of otherness. Only a full emptying of that ground could make possible its actual self-embodiment. And inasmuch as it is a full self-emptying of the ground of otherness which here occurs, and actually occurs, this must inevitably be an ultimate act of self-negation. It is ultimate in its very occurrence, for that occurrence is a full and actual realization of self-emptying. Hence it is a once-and-for-all event, an act which can never be annulled. And it can never be annulled simply because it has actually occurred. Precisely thereby lies its full actuality, an actuality which is both final and full, and final in the fullness of its realization.

Nor can a once and for all and final self-emptying be repeated or re-presented. Or not repeated in its actuality, in the actuality of its occurrence. Otherwise it could not be a once and for all and final event. An intended repetition of that event could only intend to annul its finality, and therewith to mask or dissolve its identity, its own integral and actual identity. That identity can be only its own, an identity which is actual in its uniqueness, and unique because it can happen only once. And it can happen only once just because of its fullness and finality. Simply to evoke the possibility of its repetition would be to lose its identity, to forget its actual occurrence. That loss and forgetting occur wherever actuality is evaded, or wherever that actuality is evaded which is realized by the finality of an ultimate self-emptying. That evasion occurs above all when the self-identity of this self-emptying is forgotten. And that identity is forgotten whenever the pure immediacy of actuality is lost, whenever the fullness of a self-emptying actuality regresses into a passive and disembodied state.

The actualization of self-emptying, or the self-actualization of self-negation, is the full realization of the voice and identity of "I AM." If voice realizes itself by losing itself in hearing, then so likewise the voice of "I AM" realizes itself by losing itself in its own ultimate act of self-negation. For it is precisely that act that realizes the pure actuality of "I AM," and realizes it by wholly embodying it. Now the uniqueness of the original identity of "I AM" becomes the uniqueness of the total self-embodiment of "I AM." A total self-embodiment is also thereby a total self-enactment, an enactment which is only its own, and yet just because it is its own it is ultimately actual. Even if "I AM" is embodied in its acts, and embodied in its concrete and actual acts, these acts are its own, and it is just because they are its own that they are finally actual. That finality is also an embodiment of the original finality of "I AM." But now an original finality becomes other than itself, it reverses itself, and wholly reverses itself by fully and finally emptying itself. Yet that self-emptying is the self-realization of "I AM," a self-realization which is actualized in the ultimacy of this act.

Can the self-actualization of self-negation be spoken or said? Is it spoken in the act or acts of its own self-emptying? Certainly not if speech bears the identity of its original enactment in the voice of "I AM." That speech is negated in the self-embodiment of "I AM," and negated in the immediate presence and actuality of the "Kingdom of God." But this negation is the transcendence of that original speech and voice, the self-transcendence of the voice of "I AM." Here, voice is transcended in its own act of self-actualization. Therein voice reverses itself, and passes into its own otherness. Nevertheless, voice is not silent in its otherness, or not simply and only silent. It is silent only insofar as its original voice is absent, only insofar as that voice is empty. That voice is emptied in its embodiment, in its self-embodiment, in its full actualization. But it is truly emptied not by simply being negated but rather by realizing itself in a new and final actuality. That actuality is voice itself, but it is actual as voice only insofar as the original or primal identity of voice has come to an end.

And come to an end it does in its new identity, in its self-actualization. Then its voice not only speaks by hearing, and by hearing itself, but it enacts itself in the immediacy of its act. That immediacy is speech itself, an embodied speech, a self-embodied speech, a speech which speaks only insofar as it is incarnate. Pure hearing is the incarnation of voice, an incarnation in which voice becomes totally present, and becomes totally present by ceasing to be speech and only speech. When hearing is pure, it is pure act, and when it is fully enacted it is finally enacted as a hearing which totally embodies speech. Then speech is spoken or said only insofar as it is enacted and at hand. For it is enacted by being at hand, and by being at hand in pure presence, a presence in which speech itself is totally present. Then the distance established by the pure voice of an original speech disappears, and in that disappearance an originally distant and wholly other voice is immediately at hand. At hand that is in its new voice, a voice which is its self-actualization, and its self-actualization in what is now not only a pure but also a final hearing. The finality of that hearing is the end of the original finality of pure voice, a new finality which is realized here and now and nowhere else.

Such a hearing is a final hearing because it is a final embodiment of voice. Once this embodiment has occurred, and even as it does occur, the original voice of the ground of speech becomes silent. But it is silent only by being heard. And it is fully heard in pure hearing, there its silence becomes speech, and that speech draws every hearer into itself. This occurs by virtue of the total presence of this speech, a presence in which all speech passes into hearing, and all hearing passes into speech. In this presence, or in the total presence of speech, hearing speaks whenever and wherever it hears. And it speaks because it embodies in itself the self-emptying of the primal ground of speech. This it does, and inevitably does, simply because it is hearing. As hearing, it is the otherness of speech, and it is just in that otherness that pure speech now realizes itself. Not only does pure speech now realize itself in hearing, but that realization is the self-realization of speech, a self-realization embodying the final actualization of speech.

A final actualization of speech is an incarnation of speech, and an incarnation of speech in act. Above all it is the incarnation of speech in the ultimacy and finality of act. That ultimacy is a consequence of the final self-negation of pure voice, a self-negation which is a once and for all event. Now pure voice realizes itself only in its embodiment, and that embodiment is the innermost identity of the pure immediacy of a new and final actuality. In one sense that immediacy is anonymous, for it transcends or bursts asunder all naming, all speech. Nor does it name itself, except insofar as it names itself in its hearing, in its act. This is an act which enacts itself by breaking through all speech. Now speech is speech only insofar as it is embodied in act, only insofar as it is immediately and totally present. That presence is the pure act of speech, but it is a unique act, an act released, and only released, by the full self-emptying of speech. Only a full self-emptying can embody the pure act of speech, for only that emptying can fully release the ultimate ground of speech.

That emptying enacts the advent of total presence, the total presence of speech in act. Yet the advent of total presence is both silent and invisible. Nothing apparently or manifestly distinguishes its identity from any other identity if only because the purity of its presence transcends and leaves behind all possibility of names and signs. True, it embodies the identity and thus the name of "I AM," but in the totality of this embodiment that name becomes silent. Total presence does not name itself in speech alone, and cannot do so, if only because all such naming detaches speech from act. Nor can signs of any kind point to the advent of total presence. On the contrary, signs can only disguise and veil that presence, and must do so if only because they invariably distinguish presence from absence and here from there. Once presence is present, and is totally present, absence disappears, and disappears in the totality of presence. Then nothing whatsoever can point to presence, or to pure presence, for then there can be nothing related or open to presence which is apart or distant from presence. Total presence witnesses to itself, but such witness cannot act by names and signs, it can act only by enacting itself.

While that enactment is the self-enactment of "I AM," it is nevertheless a unique enactment, and unique by virtue of the finality of its movement. Now speech ceases to be only speech, and now act ceases to be merely or only act. Speech now speaks in act, and act now acts in speech. Yet it is precisely thereby that self-identity itself is fully and finally actualized. And it is so actualized in the self-actualization of the voice and identity of "I AM." That self-actualization realizes both the purity and the totality of self-identity. Then self-identity is purely actual, and it is totally actual as well, an actuality in which identity as self-identity is totally present. But self-identity can be totally present only by embodying a total presence, and in that presence self-identity becomes identical with identity itself. Therefore no identity can stand outside of this identity, and in the presence of this identity every identity loses all that identity which is only its own. And it loses it by hearing pure presence, by hearing a presence which enacts all presence in itself, an identity whose self-identity is the identity of all actual presence.

In this pure presence, hearing and speech are one. And they are one in their enactment, in their self-enactment, a self-enactment in which act is speech and hearing at once. This is an act which draws all acts into itself, and does so insofar as they are actual and present. Indeed, the pure presence of its immediacy actualizes, and immediately actualizes, all presence. All presence, in its presence, is drawn to the immediacy of a pure but final actuality. And it is drawn to that presence by the very presence, the actual presence, of pure act. The actual presence of pure act, or its full actual presence, must also be its final presence. For act can be fully actual only by being wholly present, and it can be wholly present only by being finally present. Hence the full actuality of pure act is also its final actuality, an actuality in which act is wholly incarnate. The final actuality of pure act enacts all act, or enacts all act in its presence. But that enactment is self-enactment, a self-enactment of pure act, and a self-enactment fully embodying the voice and hearing of pure act.

That self-enactment, that final self-enactment, is the full actualization of the self-identity of pure act. Its enactment calls all identity to itself, and it calls it to itself by embodying itself, and by embodying itself in actuality. Then all self-identity, insofar as it is present and actual, is called to its own realization as the self-identity of pure act. For the call of a pure and final actuality ends every present and actual identity which is other than itself. And it ends it by calling it to itself, by calling it to its own self-actualization. In that call, and in that self-actualization, the ground of all self-identity becomes manifest as the self-identity of pure act. Now the final actuality of pure act is manifest and real as the fullness of self-identity itself. And in the pure immediacy of that actuality, every self-identity is present: "Before Abraham was, I Am."

V

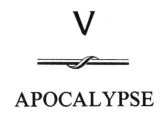

APOCALYPSE

The speech of total speech can only be the speech of total presence. But how can total presence be actually present? How can it be present in actuality? And how can it actually speak? Does it speak when voice declares: "Before Abraham was, I am"? Now the actual voice of total speech must be without a center or a source which is distant and apart. Distance disappears in total presence, and so likewise does all actual otherness which is not the otherness of that presence itself. Difference can now be present only insofar as it is fully embodied in speech. When difference speaks, and fully speaks, it becomes present in speech, and wholly present in that speech. That speech is not simply the presence of difference, or the voice of difference. It is far rather the self-identity of difference, and its fully actualized self-identity, a self-identity in which difference embodies its otherness in the immediacy of a real and actual presence. Then all otherness, or all real and actual otherness, can be actual only by being present in this voice. Thereby all actual otherness can be other only by being present, and only by being present in speech. And not only present in speech, but present as speech, as the actual voice of speech itself: "Before Abraham was, I am."

When voice says, and fully says, "Before Abraham was, I am," difference becomes present, and becomes fully present both in and as "I am." Speech now speaks in difference, and as difference as well, a difference which actually speaks. The actuality of its speech is present in the voice of "I am," a voice which now is everywhere. And it is everywhere by being spoken, by being actually spoken, and thereby by being actually present. But when difference is so present, difference is also nowhere, for nowhere can it now be only itself. That nowhere releases difference so that it is everywhere. Yet it is actually everywhere only in its full actuality as being nowhere. Hence difference as difference becomes unsaid when it is fully spoken. But it is unsaid only in being actually unsaid. The silence of the unsaid is now actually spoken, and when it is fully spoken it passes into total speech. Total speech can only be the disembodiment, the actual negation, of difference. When speech is fully embodied in pure voice, it is disembodied from difference, or disembodied from all difference which is only difference. But that disembodiment from difference is also the full actualization of difference. Now difference is fully actual by having come to an end as difference, by having come to an end as a difference which is other and apart.

All actual otherness is now an embodied otherness, and an immediately embodied otherness, an otherness which is both immediately and totally present. But it is present only insofar as actual otherness has been transcended and left behind. Then actual otherness is without either a center or a ground. For both its center and its ground have been spoken, have passed into speech. In being spoken they are self-actualized, and self-actualized in the self-identity of pure voice. Thus pure voice is the self-actualization of all actual otherness, a self-actualization in which all actual otherness is totally and immediately present. But it is so present only insofar as its difference as difference has come to an end, only insofar as that difference has become fully and totally embodied in speech. Total speech is a pure embodiment of all actual difference, and it speaks that difference by bringing a final end to silence. Silence comes to a final end when its otherness as silence is fully and finally spoken. Then the otherness of silence, that otherness which is the otherness of speech, becomes unspeakable. Yet it becomes unspeakable only by being spoken. Only by being spoken can it undergo an actual end, an end which becomes final in total speech.

Pure silence is spoken, and fully spoken, only when it comes to an end. This end is an actual end, and a purely actual end, an end which is purely actual because it is final. The finality of this end can reside only in its act, a pure act, and therefore a self-enacting act. A self-enacting act, insofar as it is actual and embodied, is a self-transcending act. And a finally self-enacting act is a finally self-transcending act. Yet it can be so only insofar as self-identity undergoes an ultimate self-transcendence, a pure act of self-transcendence wherein all self-identity which is only itself comes to a final end. All self-identity which is only self-identity comes to an end in total speech, and it comes to an end because it is spoken. The speech of total speech is itself a self-transcendence of all self-identity. And not only a self-transcendence but a final self-transcendence, an ultimate self-transcendence in which the difference of self-identity becomes wholly other than itself. This it does in its act, its own act, an act in which it fully and finally speaks. Then the silence, or the otherness, of self-identity comes to an end.

Silence ends when it is spoken, and it actually ends only inasmuch as it is spoken, only insofar as it embodies and enacts itself. Thus silence can fully end only insofar as it finally enacts itself. This occurs when silence itself becomes its own other, when it fully enacts itself in speech. Silence must enact itself if it is actually to come to an end. For only self-enactment is full actualization. Full actualization, or pure actualization, must embody the totality of itself. That totality, as totality, and its own totality, can be enacted only by itself. Not only must it be enacted by itself, but it must be totally enacted by itself, a self-enactment embodying the totality of self-identity. Yet silence can embody self-identity only insofar as it ceases to be silence. To the extent that it is manifest and real as itself, as its own self-identity, silence as silence is coming to an end. The very advent of the self-identity of silence marks the end of silence itself. Such an advent is the self-actualization of silence, a self-actualization in which silence speaks, and in which silence speaks as voice.

The voice of silence is the self-actualization of silence insofar as silence is enacting its own end. That self-enactment is a pure act, a self-negating act, an act whereby silence actually empties itself. And it empties itself in its own act, its own speech, its own voice. The voice of silence is the self-negation of silence, a negation in which silence actually empties and embodies itself. Silence hears itself when it empties itself, and it hears itself in its own speech, its own voice. That hearing is the self-actualization of silence, an actualization because it is heard, and a self-actualization because it hears itself. But it hears itself only by becoming other than itself, and it fully hears itself only by becoming wholly other than itself. That occurs in the actuality of its otherness from itself, the actuality of its difference from itself. In that difference, and in the actuality of that difference, silence realizes itself by ending itself. Thereby silence ends as the otherness of speech, and its final ending is the total embodiment of speech.

A hearing that hears the end of silence is a hearing that enacts the ending of itself. The passivity of hearing ends as hearing fully enacts itself, and it ends because that enactment is a self-enactment, an enactment in which act is real only insofar as it is self-enacted. Accordingly, it is real only inasmuch as it enacts the ending of the silence of itself. That end is the end of a hearing which is not yet fully act, and it is also thereby the end of a hearing which is not yet fully speech. But this can occur only insofar as hearing ends itself, and ends itself in its own act. This ending occurs with the diminution of silence, a diminution in which silence is progressively spoken, and is progressively spoken by being increasingly heard. But it is increasingly heard only insofar as silence is actually present, only insofar as the voice of silence is present and at hand. And at hand it is when hearing realizes itself, when hearing enacts the ending of itself.

Hearing ends itself by ever increasingly responding to the presence of silence, and to the actual presence of silence, a presence in which silence is actual because it is at hand. The actuality of silence is realized in hearing, and realized in that hearing which hears silence as dawning here, and as dawning in the act of hearing itself. The dawning of silence is the initial moment of the actual and immediate presence of silence. That moment calls attention to itself, but it does so only by way of its annulment of the unsayability of silence. Silence dawns by becoming speakable, and it becomes speakable in the fully realized act of hearing. Thereby silence becomes ever progressively unhearable as silence. Yet it is precisely by its being unhearable as silence that silence is actually heard. Once silence is actually unhearable, as it is in its dawning, then it is heard everywhere. For once it is actually unhearable, then silence is everywhere where there is hearing, everywhere where hearing is actual and real. Only the actual presence of the unhearability of silence can release hearing so that it can fully hear. And only its presence makes possible a hearing which ends itself in its own act.

As hearing hears silence, and hears the actual presence of silence, it ever increasingly hears itself as silence, and hears itself as an actual silence. Now an actual silence passes into the center of hearing, and as it does so everything within that center which is individual and apart is emptied of its ground. But it is not passively emptied of its ground, and this because hearing actually hears the actual presence of silence. Hearing enacts itself in hearing the actuality of silence and that self-enactment brings the center of hearing to an end. For the actuality of silence dawns immediately at the center of hearing, and its presence calls that center out of itself, out of its self-identity. An actual and immediate silence cannot simply enter self-identity, it is enacted by self-identity, and that self-enactment brings an end to the self-identity which is unaffected by the actual presence of silence. Then self-identity embodies the actuality of silence, and embodies it in itself, a self-embodiment wherein self-identity ever more fully actualizes itself as silence. And not simply as silence, but rather as an actually present silence, a silence which is ever active and real.

The self-embodiment of an actually present silence releases self-identity from its ground and source. Now self-identity can be active and real only insofar as it enacts its groundlessness. That self-enactment draws the presence of the actuality of silence into the center of self-identity. Then self-identity can be active and real only insofar as it actually silences itself. Moreover that silencing cannot be a mere inactivation or diminution of speech. It is far rather a movement or a process in which speech actively and actually silences itself. For the immediate presence of the actuality of silence activates rather than disengages speech, it acts upon it by entering into its very center. Then an actual silence is present at the center of speech, and speech can speak only by enacting silence. Or speech can now speak only by enacting the actual and present silence of its own self-identity. And that self-identity does not thereby become simply silent, it rather becomes actual and real insofar as it empties itself of its own speech.

Now hearing is the full actualization of the self-emptying of speech, a self-emptying in which self-identity empties itself of that which is most inherently and immediately its own. But this it can do only by passing into silence, into the actuality of silence, into an immediately actual silence. Such a silence is far other than an eternally present silence, for it is an actual and active silence, a silence which is present in its act. That act immediately enacts itself, and it enacts itself when it is heard, thereby releasing a hearing which realizes its own self-identity in the self-embodiment of silence. Then hearing hears silence whenever and wherever it actually hears, whenever and wherever it is actual and real. Indeed, it then hears silence to the extent that it hears, as its own act of hearing now empties every presence of all that identity which is embodied in speech. All identity then progressively becomes drawn into the actual silence of self-identity, as the realization of that self-identity now actually and actively unsays all the naming of speech. And this unsaying is not the mere cessation of speech. It is far rather an unsaying which acts in its silencing, and acts by disembodying all those identities in its horizon which are embodiments of speech.

Act itself now realizes itself as unsaying, as the unsaying of speech, and it does so whenever and wherever it is fully actual and real. While this unsaying is an actual disembodiment of speech, it is nevertheless an act of speech itself, an act in which speech unsays itself. But speech can truly unsay itself only in the actuality of speech. This occurs when silence speaks, and speaks in the fullness of the act of speech itself. Thereby the full self-enactment of speech becomes speech's silencing of itself. And this can only be an actual and active silencing, as self-enactment fully realizes itself in self-silencing. However, such self-silencing is not simply self-diminution. Nor is it an inactivation or dissolution of self-identity. It is far rather a real and actual self-negation or self-emptying, a self-emptying realizing itself in the actuality of its own act. And while this act is silencing, it is not silent. Nor can it be, for this is the act of speech itself, even if it is an act whereby speech silences itself. In this act, silence is truly act, and thereby it ceases to be silent.

Silence truly comes to an end only insofar as that end is actually enacted. For the end of silence can be actual and real only when that end is an actual ending. And it does actually end in the self-emptying of speech, a self-emptying in which silence becomes totally present because it is totally spoken. In that act, speech not only unsays itself, but unsays itself by way of a total act. This act draws all presence to itself, and to itself as act. All presence is enacted in this act, and enacted as the self-enactment of self-silencing. Now presence becomes absence, and becomes actual as absence, and that absence is the self-enactment of presence. Therefore presence can now be actual only in its absence, in its absence from itself, from its own self-identity. But that absence is both a real absence and a real act. Not only is it a real act, it is an act realizing all act, and it realizes all act in this act. Consequently, all self-identity is realized in this act: "The door is I."

"The door is I" when "I am the door." Yet this is a door opening to nowhere, to nowhere that is where identity is present as itself. And it opens to nowhere because its opening itself is all actual identity, all self-identity, all "I." So it is that this opening is a closing of all presence. Presence is closed in the ending of silence, in the final ending of silence, an ending which is the beginning of the absence of presence from itself. Once silence is no more, or once it has come to an actual and final end, then presence is no more as a presence which is itself. For the final ending of silence ends the self-identity of presence, or ends its ground, a ground without which presence cannot be itself as presence. No longer is presence other than absence, and no longer is speech other than silence. Now speech is speech only by its self-enactment of silence, and presence is present only by its self-enactment of absence. In that self-enactment presence loses itself as presence, and it actually loses itself by realizing itself as absence. "I am the door" only when "The door is I."

This loss of presence silences all that speech whereby identity realizes itself as presence. Now speech can speak only when identity is absent, only when it is not itself. And identity is not itself when it is present only in its absence, when its speech can embody only the absence of itself. That absence now lies at the center of speech itself, as the silence of speech is now a self-embodiment of the self-emptying of speech. Such silence speaks, and it speaks insofar as presence is actually absent, or inasmuch as absence is actually present. This occurs not simply in the disappearance of presence, but rather in the disappearance of the self-identity of presence. And this can occur only in the act of that self-identity, an act in which self-identity actually speaks, and in which it speaks by actualizing itself as silence. Now the silence of self-identity is everywhere, but it is actually everywhere only by way of the actuality of its speech, a speech in which self-identity actually realizes its own silence.

That silence which is the self-identity of speech is the fullness of speech itself. But speech can be fully realized in silence only when silence is spoken everywhere, and actually spoken everywhere, a speaking in which silence as silence wholly disappears. And it disappears in being spoken, it comes to an end in its embodiment, an embodiment in which the emptiness of silence becomes actually and immediately present. Yet this occurs only when self-identity silences itself, and only where self-identity silences itself. The self-silencing of self-identity can occur only once, but once it occurs, and in its occurrence, it occurs everywhere, and occurs everywhere where self-identity is fully actual and present. Now self-identity is self-silencing, and is so whenever and wherever it is present. For now self-identity can be present only in its absence, only in its actual absence from itself. In the silence of that absence, and only in that silence, self-identity is actually and finally itself: "The door is I."

Finally, self-identity can be itself only in silence, a silence which is actual, and a silence which is enacted in speech. That silence which is the final self-enactment of self-identity is a silence which actually dawns, which actually occurs. And it occurs in its enactment, in that act and in those acts wherein speech silences itself. Speech cannot actually silence itself simply by ceasing to speak. It can actually silence itself only by its own act, a real act, and an act in which speech is itself even in its negation of itself. Just as speech is a unique and integral realization of self-identity, then so likewise the self-silencing of speech is a unique and integral act of self-realization. And act it is in its enactment, an act or acts in which speech enacts its own end. That end is both the final end and the final realization of self-identity. Its very advent enacts the ending of all that speech whereby identity is fully and only itself. With that ending, identity can speak, and can actually speak, only by negating itself, only by silencing itself. Yet that silencing is real, and is real in its speech, a speech which negates itself insofar as it speaks.

But it does not simply negate itself in speech. Speech finally enacts itself as silence in actuality, and fully and finally enacts its silence in actuality. Then silence is embodied in every actual presence, and every actual presence is an enactment of silence. And not only an enactment, but a self-enactment, a self-enactment whereby the actuality of presence is inevitably the self-actualization of silence. The presence of that silence is a self-embodying presence, a presence calling all presence to itself, and thereby calling all presence to its own self-actualization, one whose fullness can be realized only in the actuality of silence. That fullness has been realized in the actuality of silence, has become incarnate in the finality of self-silencing, and is realized, and is now realized, wherever presence becomes fully actual and immediate. And it becomes fully actual because it has been fully actual, and finally actual, a finality which is total simply because it has occurred. That finality is total in its very occurrence, is total just because it has occurred. Therefore its occurrence occurs even now, and occurs wherever presence is fully itself.

But it can be so only where presence is absence everywhere but where it immediately and actually occurs. Indeed, the silence of that absence is the speech of an actual and immediate presence. Apart from that silence, speech could not totally speak. And once speech has totally spoken, it must henceforth be silent to continue to speak. Silent that is in its evocation of presence, in its evocation of a presence which is anywhere but here. Thereby all presence which is absent, or which is not immediately at hand, comes to an end in total presence. Total presence is total speech, but speech is total only when it is silent, only when it silences every presence that is not immediately present. That silencing occurs wherever presence is immediate and actual, and occurs because silence has actually spoken, and immediately spoken in its own voice. Once that voice has spoken, and has fully and finally spoken, then presence is silence. Presence is then silence because presence has been silenced, and having once been silenced it even now is silence, and is and will be silence wherever presence is fully actual and real.

A fully self-actualized presence can only be a total presence, and a presence in which speech and silence are one. A total speech must also and necessarily be a total silence, an actually total silence, a silence which is empty of every partial or isolated expression of speech. Not until these expressions of speech have passed into silence, or have enacted their own final silence, can presence be total or can speech and silence be one. Yet speech and silence are one in the final self-emptying of speech. In that act, and in its enactment, and its reenactment, silence speaks in speech itself because now speech can speak only by embodying a pure negation of itself in its very act of speech. In this act, in its enactment and reenactment, actuality is wholly self-actualized, and is wholly self-actualized because it wholly enacts itself. And it wholly enacts itself by wholly realizing the immediate actuality of total presence. That is the presence, and the one and only presence, in which self-realization is total actualization, an actualization in which presence is both total and is actually at hand: "The resurrection and the life are I."

"I am the resurrection and the life" only when life and death are one, only when speech and silence are united. But speech and silence are united only in their enactment, only in that self-enactment in which speech passes into silence and silence passes into speech. Speech is silence in being enacted, in being wholly enacted, or in being self-enacted. Only by wholly passing into silence does speech fully realize itself, and this speech does when it wholly enacts itself, thereby becoming both the fullness and the purity of act itself. When speech is fully realized as speech, it is purely actual as silence, and in that actuality speech is speech only inasmuch as it is actual as silence. Resurrection is the voice of speech only when that voice is actual as silence, only when the voice of speech has passed into silence. The voice of silence is the voice of resurrection, but that voice can speak only in its enactment of silence, only insofar as silence becomes fully actual and immediately at hand. And at hand it is in its enactment, in its self-enactment, a self-enactment in which speech wholly passes into silence. "The resurrection and the life are I" only when the purity of speech has passed into the actuality of silence, only when "I" has wholly enacted its own silence.

"I am" only wholly enacts its own silence by finally bringing an end to the speech of "I AM." Then the voice of silence is the voice of speech only insofar as the self-identity of speech has come to an end. Or, rather, the voice of silence is the voice of speech when the voice of speech has passed into silence. This can occur only by way of an actual end of the voice of speech. An actual end is an actual ending, a real ending of the voice of "I AM." That real ending is the silencing of "I AM," the self-silencing of "I AM," a self-silencing whereby "I AM" passes into "I am." Then "I am" is voice only insofar as it embodies the silence of the voice of "I AM." And that silence is an embodied silence, an enacted silence, a self-enacted silence, a silence which is act because it is enacted, and pure act because it is finally and totally enacted. Now speech is total because it is totally embodied, and it is totally embodied because a speech which is only speech has come to an end, and actually and finally come to an end.

That ending is not only enacted by the voice of "I am," it is heard by that voice as well, and heard insofar as it is enacted. When speech passes into silence, hearing is not only the hearing of silence, it is a reenactment or reembodiment of the passage of speech into silence. Then hearing not only speaks when it fully hears, it recapitulates or reenacts the full movement of speech itself. Such recapitulation or reenactment is not simply a repetition of speech. Nor is it a resaying of speech. It is far rather a rebirth of speech, a resurrection of speech, a new life of speech, a life in which speech is speech only insofar as it is resurrected. Speech can be resurrected only by having come to an end as speech, only by having passed into silence. And the resurrection of speech can be actual and real only to the extent that speech has actually and fully become silence. The actual silencing of speech is the portal to the resurrection of speech, and the self-silencing of speech is the door of that resurrection. Hearing is the opening of that door, and the door is opened when speech is totally heard: "The door is I."

"The door is I" when "I am the resurrection and the life." Then the voice of "I AM" is heard in the voice of "I am." That hearing is the resurrection of the voice of "I AM," but it is so only insofar as "I AM" is silent in "I am," or only insofar as the voice of resurrection is the voice of silence. When the voice of resurrection is the voice of silence, then the presence of speech is totally at hand, and totally at hand in the actuality of silence. Now silence is not only the embodiment of speech, it is the full actuality of speech, and the total actuality of speech, an actuality embodying all presence, and embodying all presence in the fullness and finality of silence. When all presence is embodied in silence, then silence is all in all, and silence is all in all when it is both actually and totally heard. A full and actual hearing of silence is not only a hearing of silence, it is an enactment of silence, and a real enactment of an actual silence. That enactment does not simply make silence present, it brings an end to all that distance established by speech, and now that distance is resurrected in the immediate and total presence of speech, a presence which can be present only in silence. But in that presence actuality is immediately at hand, and at hand in all actual presence, a presence which is presence just because it is silent, and is actual just because it is heard.

Hearing becomes pure, and realizes its own purity, as it reenacts the movement of speech as speech passes into silence. When speech realizes itself in silence, and fully realizes itself in silence, it is fully embodied in hearing. Thereby hearing becomes a resurrection of speech, as speech is reborn in silence, and reborn so that its voice becomes all in all. Then the impassable distance established by the fullness of speech passes into the total presence of a wholly actual silence. But the real movement of speech into silence, or the actual descent of the voice of speech into the voice of silence, is an absolutely necessary ground for the advent of resurrection. Apart from that ground, resurrection could be neither actual nor real. Yet once that ground has truly established and realized itself, resurrection is its inevitable culmination, a resurrection wholly embodying the pure voice of speech in the actuality of silence. Only when the voice of speech has wholly passed into the voice of silence can resurrection occur, but resurrection does occur in the advent of the voice of silence, and with the full actualization of silence resurrection dawns in all actual presence. But it can so dawn only insofar as it truly activates silence, only insofar as it brings the stillness and passivity of silence to an end.

That end is realized in the movement of speech into silence, a movement whereby the act of speech is enacted in silence, and enacted so as to actualize silence itself. Only the act of speech can actualize silence, but when speech is fully and finally enacted in silence, silence is thereby actualized, and so actualized that it can never again be only silence. Or it can never again be heard as only silence, never again be present and actually present as a silence which is only silence. Once a fully actualized silence dawns, it dawns again and again, and dawns so as to draw all actual silence into itself. Thereby the descent of speech into silence is ever again renewed, renewed and resurrected even now, and resurrected now because it once fully and finally occurred. Once speech has fully perished as speech, or has finally perished as a speech which is only speech, then speech is resurrected wherever hearing occurs, or wherever hearing is fully actual and real. That hearing is real now, is actual now, and is actual wherever actuality is immediately at hand.

And at hand it is in our silence, in a fully actualized silence, in a silence in which distance and otherness are no more. The otherness of silence disappears and is reversed when silence is fully actual and immediate in its presence. Such silence is grace, the one grace that is possible in actual presence, and it is a grace that is everywhere in the actuality of total presence. But it can be present only in the silence of voice, only when voice has passed into silence, and only as voice passes into silence. Indeed, only as our voice passes into silence is grace present to us. Yet it is present to us, present and actual to us, because pure voice has passed into total silence. The self-silencing of voice is self-actualized in silence, a silence that is present and actual whenever voice actually passes into silence. And voice does pass into silence because voice has passed into silence. Even if it happened fully and finally only once, it occurs again and again, and once again occurs even now because of the finality of that once and for all event. And it does occur even now, and even occurs to us, and occurs when we say: "It is finished."

Can we say, "It is finished"? Surely we cannot, for in the presence of this event we can say nothing. But can we hear this affirmation? Perhaps it would be wiser to ask if we can hear these words as affirmation. Do they release us from the power and the presence of all identity and all speech which is distant and other? Do they promise a total presence for us? And an actually total presence? Surely they do if we can hear them, and we do hear them because they have been said. Not only have they been said, they have been actually said, and thereby they have been enacted. Their very saying is their enactment, for they can be said only by a resurrected speech, a speech in which speech itself is finished. The real ending of speech is the dawning of resurrection, and the final ending of speech is the dawning of a totally present actuality. That actuality is immediately at hand when it is heard, and it is heard when it is enacted. And it is enacted in the dawning of the actuality of silence, an actuality ending all disembodied and unspoken presence. Then speech is truly impossible, and as we hear and enact that impossibility, then even we can say: "It is finished."